HOT AIR BALLOON

HISTORY, EVOLUTION and GREAT ADVENTURES

WHITE STAR PUBLISHERS

HOT AIR BALLOON

HISTORY, EVOLUTION and GREAT ADVENTURES

foreword by BERTRAND PICCARD

preface by ROBERTO MAGNI ● DANIELA COMI

text by JEAN BECKER

photographs by ROBERTO MAGNI ● DANIELA COMI

project editor VALERIA MANFERTO DE FABIANIS

editorial coordination LAURA ACCOMAZZO ● GIORGIO FERRERO

graphic design PAOLA PIACCO ● MARIA CUCCHI

contents

1 A BALLOON ADVERTISES A WELL KNOWN BRAND OF TIRES.

2-3 THE "FINANCIAL TIMES" DELIVERED HOME IN OCCASION OF THE BIENNIAL CHAMBLEY MEETING, IN FRANCE, WHICH TAKES PLACE IN AUGUST IN THE VICINITIES OF METZ.

4-5 THE COLORS OF A HOT-AIR BALLOON VIEWED FROM ANOTHER BALLOON AS THEY FLY OVER FRENCH FIELDS.

foreword

BERTRAND PICCARD

The balloon is known as the device that first enabled humans to fly, but it is also the symbol of a different relationship that humans developed with nature and with themselves. Propelled by the wind, with no engine and no rudder, the pilot of a balloon must learn to surrender his or her own need to control and dominate. In this sense, the balloon is a metaphor for life.

Indeed, it can be said that much of mankind's suffering in life derives from the deep-rooted human need to be in control. It is difficult to accept that life can lead us in a direction that differs from that dictated by our will. In this sense, flying a balloon forces us to admit that our will is powerless in the face of the blowing wind. A certain degree of skill is necessary, but only in relation to controlling what is in our power to control. In reality, a balloon pilots' only degree of freedom is limited to modifying the flying altitude in order to find other wind directions. The same happens in life: the only way to change direction when the winds of life are unfavorable is to change altitude, to rise psychologically and philosophically to capture other influences, ideas, solutions or answers. In this way we can find new skills and interior resources, new ways of thinking, to adapt to the unforeseeable events of life.

It is for this reason, as with balloons, that we must learn to throw out the ballast. Of course in life it would not be sand, but certainties, habits, prejudices and dogmas of all types. Everything, in other words, that keeps us prisoner to our old ways of thinking, in bad directions.

And so, on every page of this magnificent book you can ask yourself what could be the best height to reach in your life and which ballast you should learn to throw out so that you can set off in the direction you want.

Enjoy the book and, above all, fair winds!

6-7 *THE DELIGHTFUL SHAPES AND COLORS OF THE BALLOONS INSPIRE PHOTOGRAPHERS TO TAKE STRIKING AND CAPTIVATING PHOTOGRAPHS.*

9 *A BALLOON IN THE SHAPE OF A HOUSE RISES INTO THE SKY ABOVE ALBUQUERQUE.*

10-11 *BERTRAND PICCARD AT THE PRESS CONFERENCE FOR THE FIRST SOLAR IMPULSE AIRPLANE PROTOTYPE, HB-SIA, NOVEMBER 2007.*

12-13 AT THE ALBUQUERQUE FESTIVAL THE MASS ASCENSIONS HAVE ALWAYS BEEN IMPRESSIVE DUE TO THE HUNDREDS OF BALLOONS THAT TAKE PART.

preface

ROBERTO MAGNI - DANIELA COMI

It is said that a thousand years ago some Irish monks allowed themselves to be transported adrift on a boat without oars, at the mercy of the prevailing currents. Wherever the sea took them, they disembarked and preached. Centuries later came the Montgolfier brothers, who showed for the first time that mankind could also sail in the sky and that the currents could be governed. Their ascents, achieved under the incredulous gaze of curious crowds, even captured the imagination of poets. The same emotion is generated today in the gaze of a photographer who, suspended from a rising balloon, can see houses and villages getting smaller and smaller while the wind guides it through casual paths. The balloon is not like a leaf that the wind drags away; the drift is controlled and there is a really beautiful balance that changes from moment to moment, between the world below and the gondola. Trustingly, you allow yourself to be transported by a breeze or strong wind because you know that you can always decide to land whenever you want. But the beauty of the game lies in prolonging as long as possible that fragile, dynamic, rocking balance between the balloon and the ocean of winds. When you are up there all movements are gentle and smooth, accentuating the sensation of being a part of the whole, gentle elements of the universe in harmony with nature. When we fly we feel the need to freeze those fleeting moments into images that will later recall the sense of peace and freedom we feel when we are face to face with infinity, the constant readjustment of equilibrium with every slight modulation of the wind. No longer constrained by the force of gravity, we take photographs and abandon ourselves to continuous emotions. From that undulating perspective, you can make out, as you would on a giant screen, a village emerging from the mist, and following the clouds we can see valleys and hills coming into view one after another. In the wake of the wind, the tidy lines of balloons are photographed. Some pictures emphasize colors or highlight the transparency of the balloons, while others are evocative landscapes. The fragments of world imagery that emerge are like distant islands that momentarily suspend thoughts and actions before changing direction. Our photographs are like anchors thrown in the harbors of the sky to freeze unrepeatable moments. In each one of these pictures are rhythms, colors, emotions, the wake of a flame that warms up and beats like a heart. Visions captured between an ascent and a descent, pictures that always arouse an almost irresistible urge to go up, up and away ... and fly. Always.

14-15 MARTIAL, THE PILOT
OF "BALLOONING
ADVENTURES," FLIES OVER
NORWEGIAN LAPLAND
IN MARCH 2000 DURING
THE FIRST BALLOON CROSSING
OF THE REGION.

introduction

SCENT OF ADVENTURE

Since time immemorial humans have traveled to discover new lands, but according to the new explorers of the 21st century it is harder now to discover unknown territories. However, thanks to the hot-air balloon, adventurers can now journey through lands in a friendly and non-intrusive way. Although I am not comparing ourselves to the great travelers of the past, such as Marco Polo or Christopher Columbus, by means of our balloons, at the mercy of the winds, we are welcomed in the most isolated countries as friendly visitors from the sky. And thanks to our delightful mode of transport, even if the inhabitants of a region do not usually like unexpected visits, they will greet us with open arms. This has happened with people in Lapland, Berbers in Morocco, Bedouins in Jordan, and even the Apache and the Navajo of New Mexico. The balloonist still fascinates old and young alike, and for this reason sponsors are very interested in participating with these great trips.

We like to believe that it is the dangerous but noble desire to see what lies beyond the horizon that motivates these new adventurers. And daring and brave adventurers they really are when they pilot their craft over great distances. After a competition or taking passengers for flights, a pilot often feels a certain tedium. He or she feels the need for some freedom, such as taking a hot-air balloon to a region where no-one has ever attempted to fly one before. Ballooning arouses in the hearts of men and women an irresistible need to embark on an adventure. These remarkable airships seem to carry inside them, like a light or a flame, something that ignites the imagination of generations of explorers. There may be few if any new regions to explore, but from a balloon you see the world in a completely different and novel way. The challenges are innumerable and our ambitions become greater each year.

For the first ever Chateau-d'Oex International Hot Air Balloon Week, the committee looked for a "godfather," a personality of a certain type, able to establish the meeting and in particular to

16 LEFT IN JULY 2000 THE FRENCH CREW OF "BALLOONING ADVENTURES" FLEW OVER THE GREAT SWEDISH LAKES IN THE GRÄNNA REGION, THE BIRTHPLACE OF AUGUSTE ANDRÉ, WHO MADE THE FIRST ATTEMPT TO REACH THE NORTH POLE IN A GAS BALLOON.

16 RIGHT THE BALLOON OF THE CITY OF RHEIMS DURING THE WORLD HOT AIR BALLOON CHAMPIONSHIP IN SAGA, JAPAN (NOVEMBER 1989). THE BALLOON WAS PILOTED BY JEAN BECKER.

17 FOR KING HUSSEIN OF JORDAN'S 40TH ANNIVERSARY, IN NOVEMBER 1992, ROYAL JORDANIAN AIRLINES ORGANIZED A BALLOONING COMPETITION IN THE DESERT AREA OF WADI RUM IN SOUTHERN JORDAN. THE BEST PILOTS ON THE INTERNATIONAL CIRCUIT PARTICIPATED. THIS WAS ONE OF THE MOST PRESTIGIOUS DISPLAYS IN A CONTEST THAT WAS THE STUFF OF WHICH DREAMS ARE MADE.

put it on the map. The director of the Tourist Office found among the inhabitants of the small community of Pays d'Enhaut just the person. An international film star who had played the role of Phileas Fogg in the 1956 film *Around the World in 80 days* – David Niven. He inaugurated the first Hot-Air Balloon Week in 1978.

The following year his name was associated with the long-distance race, the David Niven Cup, which became a competition that pilots loved to enter. In 1983, the race was won by the late-lamented Michel Arnould, who achieved a distance of 195 miles (315 km). Sadly, in July of the same year David Niven died.

In 1994, when there had not been a French participant since Michel Arnould, along with my crew member Julien Fath, I enjoyed the experience of crossing the Alps while competing for the David Niven Cup. The attempt involved a great deal of preparation, because flying at over 20,000 ft (6000 m) requires thorough planning regarding the flight plan. It was not the first time I had entered the David Niven Cup, but previously the winds had carried me to France or Switzerland. In 1992, together with Gérard Scherer as a crew member, we found ourselves in the region of Arc-et-Senans and we reached an altitude of 26,000 ft (8000 m), with a temperature of -43.6°F (-42°C).

At 8.30 a.m. the first balloon takes off from Château-d'Oex, carrying 350 lbs (160 kg) of propane, measurement devices, and a radio, which is necessary to communicate with the control tower of the airports in order not to disrupt air traffic. We quickly ascend to an altitude of 20,000 ft (6000 m)! We rise vertically over Gstaad and then our balloon heads toward Italy. Every 15 minutes we breathe oxygen with our masks, while the controllers in Geneva, thanks to our transponder, follow our flight on their radar screens.

At 20,000 ft (6 000 m) we encounter a N/NW wind of 55 mph (90 km/h). A cruising speed that will allow us to cross the Alps and take us right into Italy. We fly over the Sion Valley, then the winter station of Zermatt. In front of us stands the Matterhorn (14,692 ft/4478 m), which can be recognized by its pyramid shape, and to our left is Mt. Rosa (15,000 ft/4600 m). In the background and to our right stands the massive Mt. Blanc.

PARMIGIANI
SWISS WATCHES PAR EXCELLENCE
WWW.PARMIGIANI.COM
SWITZERLAND

In order to avoid the turbulence caused by the violent winds which swirl around the peaks we decide to ascend to 21,000 ft (6500 m). Here we achieve a speed of 68 mph (110 km/h) and we pass over Mt. Rosa.

We had to maintain this altitude for approximately an hour and then we arrived over the Po Valley. Finally, we landed at 12.30 p.m., 37 miles (60 km) to the south of Novara. Some Italian farmers welcomed us: champagne for all. We had traveled more than 125 miles (200 km). On this occasion the winner of the David Niven Cup covered a distance of 162 miles (262 km).

In March 2002 a team of "Ballooning Adventures," the ballooning association which I direct, chose to fly over the Norwegian Lapland with two hot-air-balloons. White as far as the eye can see. Here and there a few scattered shrubs sprouted out of the snow. Beneath us extended the splendid, vast white landscape of Lapland.

We were in the area of Kautokeino, 186 miles (300 km) north of the Arctic Circle, hoping to cross this region in a balloon for the first time. The only noise came from our burner, otherwise this was a world of silence. It was still cold and the birds had not yet returned from their distant summer habitats. We were trying to aim for a big lake, so that our ground crew would find us more easily. The sky was azure and on the horizon can be seen the Alta mountains, some hundred miles away to the north. The Norwegians call them Fjälls and we gave them the nickname of the White Mountains. Nobody ventures into this region during the winter. The Laplanders and their reindeer herds stay farther to the west. But here there is nothing – no streets, no houses, and no animals. This is the immense wildness of Lapland.

On the morning of March 25, 2002 we took off from a snow-covered road, because it was impossible to inflate the balloon in the tundra. We sank upto our waists whenever we left the snowscooter tracks or the roads. The thermometer read -13° F (-25° C), however, there was no wind to make the conditions even harsher. We were in a lunar landscape where the cold froze moustaches and nose hairs, but we wore warm clothes from head to foot. Our recovery teams were more than 30 miles (50 km) away and we continued our flight at an altitude of 3280 ft (1000 m). The silence was disturbed by the voices of our ground crew coming from the radio. From where they were they could not see the balloons and were as worried as we were. As I mentioned, the target we had chosen was a big lake formed by the Alta River, but for the moment we did not turn in that direction. We did not take our eyes off of the GPS or the altimeter in order to find the right wind direction which would take us to our desired destination. After an hour of flight we decided to ascend to 6500 ft (2000 m). At this height the team on the ground would be able to spot us as two little multicolored spots in the sky. We could see Kautokeino, our new base camp.

At 6500 ft (2000 m) the correct wind currents did not exist, so we descended steadily and at 820 ft (250 m) we finally found the right wind. After an hour and a half we arrived at the lake, where our teams would meet us on the snow scooters. When we returned to the base camp at Kautokeino, it was 1 p.m. and we had started at 4.30 a.m. We had just completed successfully the first flight of a hot-air balloon over Norwegian Lapland, and after another 11 flights we completed the first crossing of Lapland.

On the summer solstice of 2008 a team of "Ballooning Adventures" took off from the center of St. Petersburg and flew over the city in three hot-air balloons: Parmigiani, Romorantin and their mascot Cocorico. It was a great exploit and you can easily imagine the great administrative obstacles that had to be overcome in order to get permission.

We decided to take off from the Peter and Paul Fortress, which is on a small island just in the front of the Hermitage on the banks of the Neva. On the ground there was no wind, but in the air there was a good wind in the right direction, and the sky was clear and blue. Raymond with some photographers took off on board Cocorico, just before I did, and he would trail the way. Claude, in Romorantin, would follow us at a slight distance. So we were in the sky over St. Petersburg. The very first time that hot-air balloons had flown over the city and they are piloted by three Frenchmen. It was extraordinary. Fortunately, once we had reached 2300 ft (700 m) we found some wind, because we had to travel at least 18 miles (30 km) in order to get beyond the city limits.

Behind us were the waters of the Gulf of Finland, beneath us the Neva River, and before us stretching away to the horizon an immense urban area which seemed to be endless. Altogether less than dozen pilots took part in this historic flight. After an hour and a half we landed without any problems on an immense field. The most difficult thing for our recovery team would be to find a way to reach the balloon, because the map we had was not reliable, the road signs, if any, were in Russian, and it was not possible to ask the inhabitants for directions. Furthermore, as if that was not enough, the roads were unsurfaced and full of terrible holes. Our team took two hours to reach us and it took a further two hours or so to return our passengers back to their hotel in St. Petersburg. It was a Monday morning and the traffic was terrible. The St. Petersburg traffic was worse than in Paris! After this we returned to Pushkin, refuelled, had a quick breakfast, and then had a briefing at 5 p.m. Soon we began to understand the meaning of "The white nights of St. Petersburg." By the evening the weather situation had taken a turn for the worse, there were sudden storms and everywhere disturbed and unsettled conditions. Finally, we managed to get some welcome relaxation, considering that the rest of the week would be just as eventful with four additional flights over St. Petersburg. The bet had been won.

The history of balloon flying

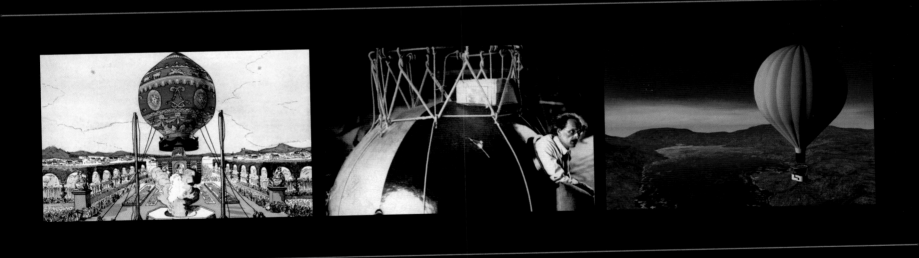

Vuë d'Annonay en Vivarais.

THE PIONEERS

On November 21, 1783 man realized an ancient dream. He rose into the air and entered the realm of the birds. The story began in 1782, in the area of Annonay, the capital city of Haut-Vivarais, France, where the Montgolfier family managed the important paper-mill of Vidalon. Pierre, the patriarch, assisted by some of his children, was a prosperous engineer and an important figure in this little world and was involved in the development of several engineering advances and inventions. Joseph (1740–1810), the second-born, had always preferred the practice to the theory, so he left school to dedicate himself to real-world experiments. Constantly absorbed in some new invention, he was often absentminded, even forgetting his wife in different hotels, however, he never forget his horse! The aerostatic balloon was his creation, but his name is linked to many other inventions as well. Joseph was gifted with a great imagination and in the course of his life he invented various devices: the hydraulic pump, machines for the cutting and production of paper, a calorimeter, and even a device for drying fruit.

Etienne (1745-1799) was a very cultured man, who desired to continue his studies in Paris, at the Soufflot school, a renowed institute, where he would attend the courses of Architecture. At the end his father ordered him to leave the capital city in order to manage the family company, the paper-mill of Vidalon.

Both Montgolfier brothers, Joseph and Etienne, who were keen on scientific researches, in the evenings discussed for a long time in the hope to create a balloon. The hydrogen and the experiments with the hydrogen excited them, and both brothers could think about nothing except about flying. They even had the idea to catch the clouds in a kind of envelope and to hang on it a basket, but they didn't know how to realise this project.

It was cold on this November day in 1782. Joseph Montgolfier was in Avignon, occupied with his business. In his room he warmed up in front of the camin and let his mind wander, while he was

looking how the smoke raised up from the fire. And here he got an idea and riflected: this smoke which is rising up towards the clouds, it is enough to catch it in a paper bag and to catch hold of it in order to leave for the conquest of the skies.

So he took a paper leaf, folded it four so that it could hold the smoke, and he posted it over the fire. The small aerostat, if it could be called so, raised up towards the throat of the camin.

Joseph had discovered the principle of the hot air balloon.

By means of a needle and thread, which he asked for to his landlady, he started to construct a cube, then he threw it in the camin and the parallelepiped raised up in the air.

For Joseph this was a victory. It is not difficult to imagine his happiness when he saw this first small aerostat rise in flight.

Joseph revealed his discovery to his brother Etienne and said to him: "Prepare a great quantity of taffeta and cords, and I will demonstrate to you the most extraordinary thing in the world!" Joseph went on foot to Annonay to discuss personally his invention. As he was walking his mind might well have figured out the craziest ideas and the most senseless hopes. In the most hidden corner of the paper-mill, the brothers began to construct prototypes. The first airship, a cube a yard in diameter,

was constructed out of very thin taffeta and silk. When it was warmed up over the fire, the cube took off and rose up rapidly to the ceiling. These first experiments marked the birth of hot air ballooning. However, the Montgolfier brothers did not stop there and began at once working on a new experiment, this time using a paper envelope.

On December 14, 1782, a sphere of 105 cu ft (3 cu m) was warmed over a fire of straw mixed with wool and paper. It rose in the air from the gardens of the Vidalon paper-mill. Until this moment they had always worked in secret in the garden of their house, but as the flights got ever higher they began to worry that the neighbors would discover their experiments and steal their idea. So they decided to organize a public flight of their aerostat in Annonay, in front of people they could trust and who could testify and certify that the invention was creation of the Montgolfier brothers. They constructed a big balloon of 31,000 cu ft (900 cu m) made up of packing cloth reinforced by triple layers of paper. In order to join the cloths they made 1800 buttonholes where cords could be inserted. On Wednesday, June 4, 1783, both brothers publicly presented their new balloon in front of the *Etats particulars* of Vivarais, which met together in the assembly in Annonay.

34 On September 19th, 1783 a balloon with a cage containing a cock, a duck and a sheep suspended under the envelope took off from the Palace of Versailles.

35 Another illustration that shows the "Réveillon," the first balloon to carry passengers, taking off from the courtyard of the Palace of Versailles in the presence of Louis XVI, on September 19th, 1783.

Experience Areostatique faite a Versailles le 19 Sept.bre 1783 en presence de leurs Majestes et de la famille Royale par M.r de Montgolfier avec un Balon de 52 pieds d'hauteur sur 41 de Diamettres. Cette Superbe machine a fond d'asur avec le Chiffre du Roi pesant 900 livres. Ce balon a été enlevé avec toutes l'aplaudissement de tout les Spectateurs et a tombé dans le Bois de Vaucresson Carrefour Marechal.

In the square in the front of the Cordeliers convent were erected two wooden poles from which was suspended the envelope to be inflated. Under the mouth of the envelope was placed a basket full of straw and wool which was set alight, and when the heat was sufficient to raise the balloon, which had an internal temperature of 189.5°F (87.5°C), on the instruction "Release everything!" the restraining ropes were cut and the balloon rose up into the air. After about a 10-minute flight it landed in Davézieux, a distance of approximately 1.5 miles (2.5 km). When it landed it caught fire and the farmers at work in the field were so scared by this strange object that had fallen from the sky that they did not try to extinguish the flames and the prototype was completely destroyed.

On June 5 the *Etats particulars* of Vivarais prepared a report containing all the details of the flight, and on July 26 Louis XVI ordered the Academy of Sciences to study the experiment. The Academy invited Etienne Montgolfier to Paris to provide a demonstration. In August 1783 Etienne met the scientists interested in his invention, in particular the young physicist Pilâtre de Rozier. Funding was provided to construct a balloon, which would carry a cockerel, a duck, and a ram. Etienne carried out his experiment in front of the Academy of Sciences. This first manned flight was planned for September 19 in the presence of Louis XVI. Before leaving Versailles, the king and his family thoroughly examined the new invention. Finally, the balloon, which was named Réveillon, for a friend of Etienne's who had offered him accommodation during his stay in Paris, rose up in the air and after an eight-minute flight landed near the Vaucresson forest. The experiment was a success and witnessed by two gamekeepers who assisted with the landing.

In the same period the physicist Jacques Alexandre Charles constructed a hydrogen balloon. Charles was a famous physicist who was interested in researching the field of gases, which had recently been established by the work of Black, Cavendish, Prestley, and Lavoisier. He started with developing experiments on the physical proprieties of gases. He studied in particular the density and the dilatation coefficient, and in this way he confirmed the results obtained by Cavendish that among the inflammable gases, hydrogen (as it would become known) was 14 times lighter than air. Charles would demonstrate its "lighter than air" qualities by inflating soap bubbles which took-off in front of his students.

He was convinced that for the demonstration of June 4, 1783, that the Montgolfier brothers had inflated their balloon with hydrogen.

He also wanted to rise a balloon into the air as part of his physics experiments. Charles contacted the brothers Anne-Jean and Marie-Noël Robert to construct a balloon of 13 ft (4 m) in diameter, which was called the Globe. It was water resistant thanks to the use of an elastic rubber, the secret of which they guarded closely. At 5 p.m. August 27, 1783, in front of an enormous crowd of Parisians, the Globe rose up from the Champ de Mars. The crowd was so large that the Duke of Richelieu's (the former marshal of France) carriage could not get through and he had to proceed on foot. Later on the balloon caused terror when it landed in the small town of Gonesse, to the north of Paris. The frightened farmers of Gonesse were convinced that this was a creation of the devil and destroyed the balloon by hitting it with pruning hooks. In order to avoid such accidents in the future, on September 3rd the government distributed a notice to the population stating that they should remain calm.

After this there developed an intense rivalry between the hot air balloon and the Charlière, as the gas balloon of Jacques Charles and the brothers Robert was known.

37 bottom When Charles' balloon landed on August 27th, 1783 near Gonesse, in the Ile-de-France region, the terrified peasants destroyed it, thinking that it was some kind of diabolical creature.

Etienne, who had already performed many attempts with bound balloons in the gardens of the paper-manufacturer Réveillon in Paris, wanted to go over and thouth already about manned flights. It started a real race with the "gaziers". However, the king did not agree and Etienne had to negotiate hard in order to realize his dream. Pilâtre de Rozier and the Marquis d'Arlandes argued his case in front of the sovereign and finally Louis XVI gave his authorization, but he refused to assist the experiment in anyway, giving the reason that he was the guarantor of his citizens.

The new aerostat was located at a construction site and had an envelope of 77,700 cu ft (2200 cu m) made of blue cotton and emblazoned with royal emblems in gold. The balloon was a real work of art. It was equipped with a circular capsule consisting of two baskets for the passengers and a central burner. On Wednesday, October 15, 1783 Pilâtre de Rozier stepped onto the balcony (*galerie*) connected to the balloon and rose up over the park to a height of over 100 ft (30 m), while tethered by ropes. On Friday, the 17th, the experiment was re-

peated and Pilâtre had the opportunity to improve his procedures. This time the balloon rached 354 ft (108 m). As the date of the first free ascent got closer the king decided that two ferocious criminals, condemned to death, should be the first passengers. If they survived the experiment, they would be pardoned, and as they were to be executed then it would not matter if they did not. When Pilâtre de Rozier was told about the king's proposal he energetically responded: "How is it possible that vile criminals, murderers who are the dregs of society, will receive the privilege to be the first navigators of the sky?" However, after a conversation with the marquis d'Arlandes and the duchess of Polignac, the king changed his mind. Finally, Louis XVI asked marquis d'Arlandes to accompany Pilâtre de Rozier.

Later all the necessary equipment was transported to Château de la Muette, from where the hot air balloon would take-off. Pierre Montgolfier had prohibited his sons from flying. As planned, on December 21, 1783 Pilâtre de Rozier and the marquis d'Arlandes got into the circular capsule for the

ascent. The balloon had an area of 72,000 cu ft (2040 cu m), was 69 ft (21 m) in length and 45 ft (14 m) wide. It rose slowly up. The envelope was made up of cotton soaked with alum in order to make it water resistant and less inflammable. Pilâtre, who had a well-developed sense of orientation, recognized the moment when the balloon should be

warmed up in order to maintain the right altitude and he steered the balloon, while the marquis d'Arlandes admired the bird's-eye view of Paris. After a flight of 25 minutes, and after having crossed the Seine and traveled for about 6 miles (10 km), the first pilots in history returned to earth without any accidents at Butte-aux-Cailles on the edge of Paris.

38 THE FRENCH SCIENTIST JEAN-FRANÇOIS PILÂTRE DE ROZIER (1756–1785) WAS THE FIRST MAN TO FLY ON BOARD A BALLOON, ON OCTOBER 15TH, 1783.

38-39 THE GARDEN OF THE PAPER MANUFACTURER, RÉVEILLON, IN RUE DU FAUBOURG SAINT-ANTOINE IN PARIS, WHERE THE MONTGOLFIER BROTHERS MADE THEIR BALLOON. THE ILLUSTRATION SHOWS THEIR TETHERED FLIGHT ON OCTOBER 11TH, 1783.

40 TOP HAVING TAKEN OFF FOR THE FIRST TIME ON BOARD A GAS BALLOON CALLED "CHARLIÈRE" ON DECEMBER 1ST, 1783, JACQUES CHARLES RETURNED TRIUMPHANT TO PLACE DES VICTOIRES WITH HIS BALLOON THE FOLLOWING DAY.

40 BOTTOM THE FIRST GAS BALLOON FLIGHT, PILOTED BY PHYSICIST JACQUES CHARLES AND BY MARIE-NOËL ROBERT, TOOK PLACE ON DECEMBER 1ST, 1783. THE 380-CUBIC METER HYDROGEN BALLOON TOOK OFF FROM THE TUILERIES GARDENS IN PARIS AND COVERED 36 KILOMETERS IN TWO HOURS.

In the meantime, the physicist Charles did not sit idly by and at the Tuileries palace he worked to produce an envelope of 13,500 cu ft (380 cu m) made of yellow-red silk, which was water resistant and had a magnificent wicker basket. Only 10 days after Pilâtre de Rozier's ascent, Jacques Charles and Marie-Noël Robert ascended from the Tuileries garden, in the very middle of Paris, in the presence of 400,000 people (about half of the total population of the city at that time). The flight lasted two hours and the balloon came to ground in Nesles-la-Vallée, some 22 miles

(36 km) away. Charles left his co-pilot on the ground and took off again alone, achieving an altitude of more than 9800 ft (3000 m) in spite of the terrible cold. He could measure the altitude by means of his barometer. When night came he landed at Tour de Leys, not far from Nesles.

Charles had designed a revolutionary gas balloon, the principles of which are still used today. His balloon used a valve, a sleeve for the discharging of the gas, a net, fixing ropes, a wicker basket, ballast, an anchor, and he also carried measuring devices.

Ce Glôbe à tombé entre Nesle et Hedouville à 9 l. de Paris, aux environs de Pontoise,

rue S. J. de Bauvais la 4.ᵉ porte cochère à droite par la rüe des Noyers

Dessiné d'après nature.

41 On December 1st, 1783, the "Charlière," the balloon invented by Charles and Robert, rose from the Tuileries Gardens in Paris. The two French passengers on board wave to the crowd with flags.

So began the real conquest of the sky, involving the most extravagant inventions in order to remain in the air for as long as possible. On January 19, 1784 in Lyon, while one ascent followed another in all the big cities of France, Pilâtre de Rozier took flight in an enormous hot air balloon of 706,000 cu ft (20,000 cu m) called the Flesselles, for the governor of the province. It carried six passengers, including Etienne Montgolfier. It was the first commercial flight. On March 2, 1784, in Paris, Jean-Pierre Blanchard ascended in a gas balloon from the Champ de Mars, and he tried to control the direction of his flight, which lasted one hour and 15 minutes, by using some palms. On April 25 and on June 12 of the same year the balloon of Dijon Academy, equipped with oars and a rudder, was tested by Guyton de Morveau, accompanied by the abbot Bertrand and afterwards by Monsieur De Virly. In Lyon, on June 4, 1784, for the first time a women took part in a flight. Elisabeth Thible was a passenger in the hot air balloon La Gustave, named in honor of King Gustav of Sweden who had assisted in funding the event.

In the following years various scientific tests and experiments were performed in order to improve the performance of hot air balloons. The next great challenge was to fly across the English Channel.

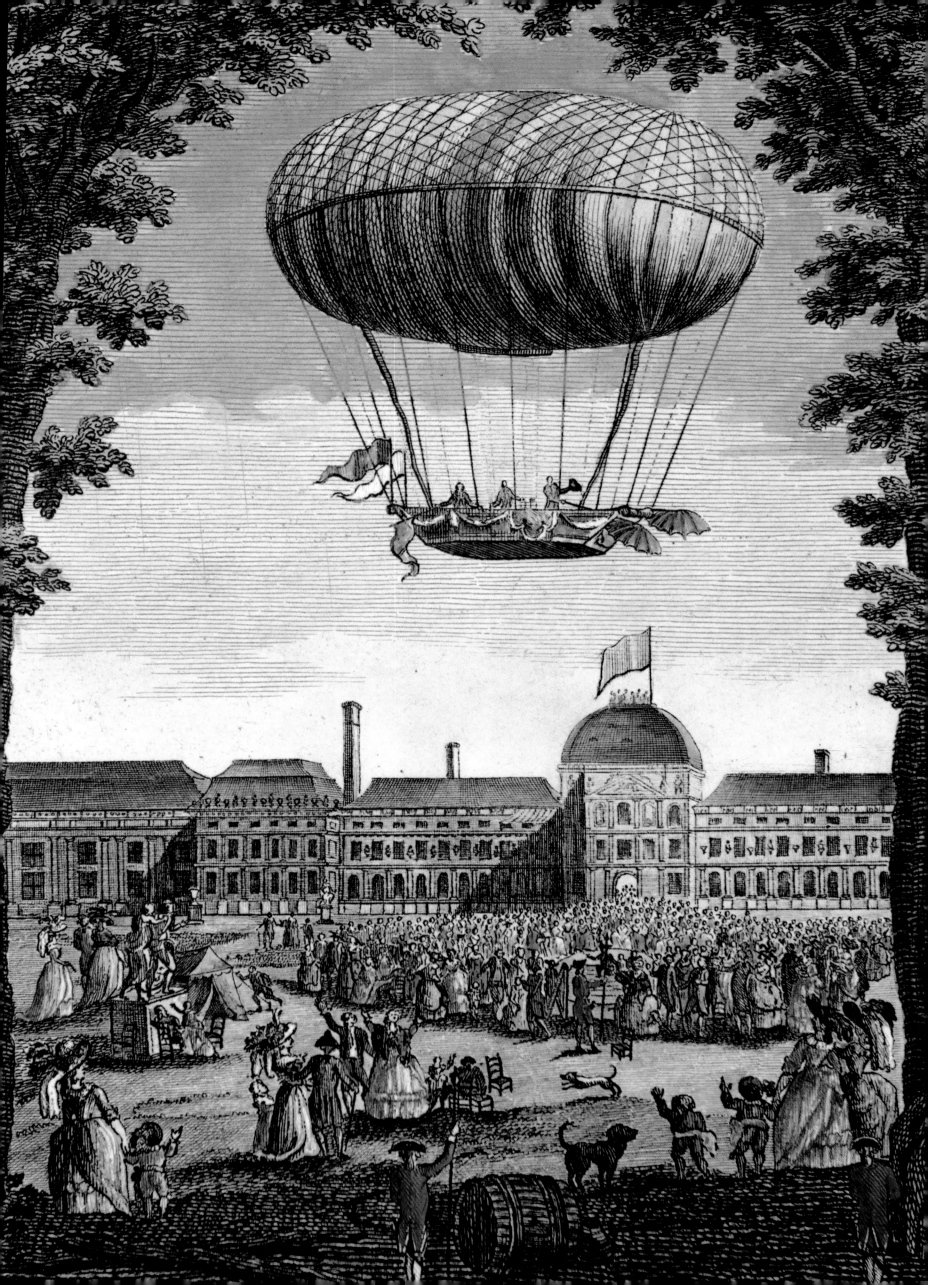

SIC ITUR   AD ASTRA

Desrais del.   Denis Scul.

EXPERIENCE DU VAISSEAU VOLANT DE MON^R. BLANCHARD
Enlevé au Champ de Mars près Paris le 2. Mars 1784. entre Midi et 2 Heures.

44 On March 2nd, 1784, at the Champs de Mars in Paris, an enormous crowd witnessed the first flight of the "Vaisseau Volant" (flying vessel), Blanchard's airship created in the shape of a bird.

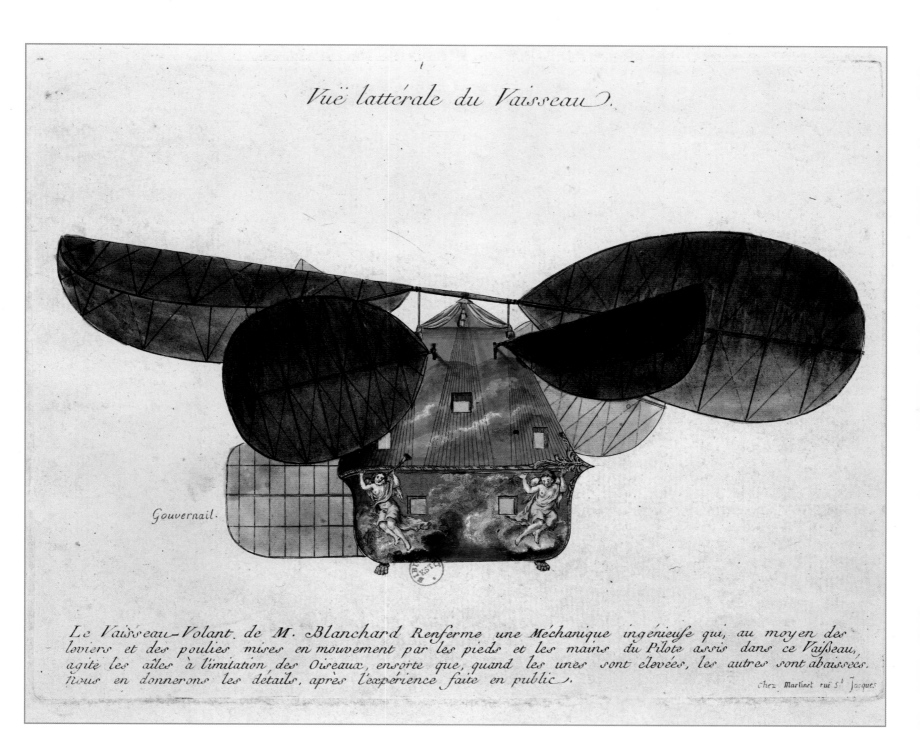

Vuë lattérale du Vaisseau.

Gouvernail.

Le Vaisseau-Volant de M. Blanchard Renferme une Méchanique ingénieuse qui, au moyen des leviers et des poulies mises en mouvement par les pieds et les mains du Pilote assis dans ce Vaisseau, agite les ailes à l'imitation des Oiseaux, ensorte que, quand les unes sont élevées, les autres sont abaissées. Nous en donnerons les détails, après l'expérience faite en public.

Chez Martinet rue S.t Jacques

45 The design of the "Vaisseau Volant" airship, a bird-shaped flying vessel with six wings and a rudder designed by French aviator Jean-Pierre Blanchard. Blanchard organized a public display on May 5th, 1782, but was unable to take off.

46 IN 1781 THE FRENCHMAN JEAN-PIERRE BLANCHARD INVENTED HIS FLYING VESSEL, POWERED BY ARMS AND LEGS.

47 ON JANUARY 7TH, 1785 JEAN-PIERRE BLANCHARD, ACCOMPANIED BY AMERICAN JOHN JEFFRIES, CROSSED THE ENGLISH CHANNEL ON BOARD A BALLOON WITH A GONDOLA EQUIPPED WITH "WIND OARS." THE TWO AERONAUTS WERE CONVINCED THAT THE OARS WOULD FACILITATE THE FORWARD MOVEMENT AND THE STEERING OF THE BALLOON BUT THE AEROSTAT FLEW AT THE SAME SPEED AS THE WIND AND THE OARS WERE RENDERED COMPLETELY USELESS.

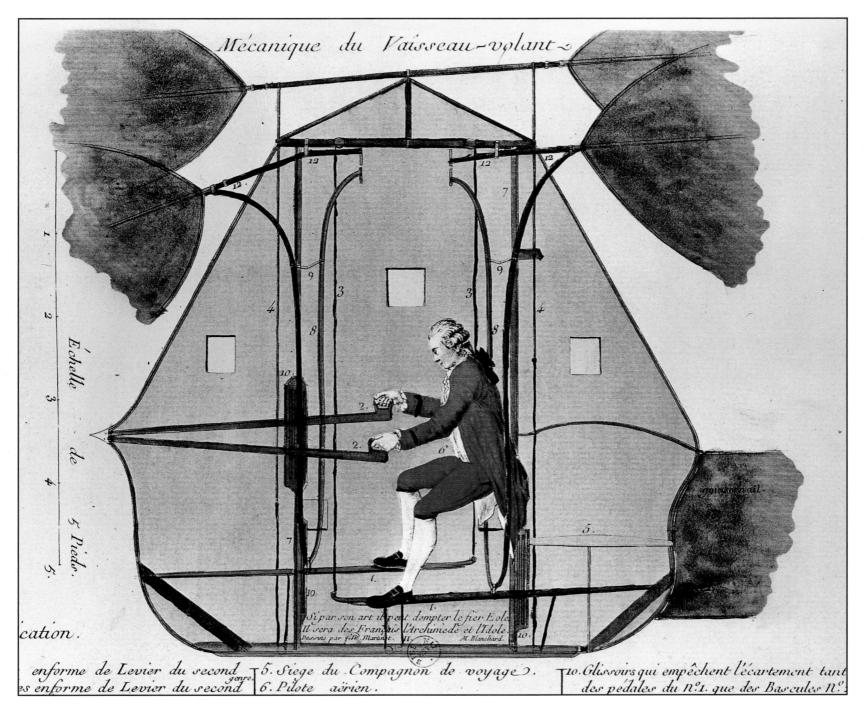

A new competition between hot air and gas began. At this point there appeared a gas-balloon pilot, the engineer Jean-Pierre Blanchard. He was already known as an inventor of special hydraulic machinery, a penny-farthing bicycle, and a steam coach. Following the successes of Montgolfier and Charles, Blanchard decided to dedicate himself to balloon flight. On January 7, 1785, accompanied by an American doctor, John Jeffries, who was his patron, he took off from London and crossed the English Channel in a gas balloon. To succeed they had to throw into the sea many parts of the balloon, including its huge propellers, all the instrumentation, and even their money in order to avoid sinking beneath the waves. Eventually, they landed not far away from the Guînes forest in France.

Pilâtre de Rozier had also announced his intention to cross the English Channel and he designed a new balloon. However, this great pilot from Lorraine, who had already broken all altitude records in his hot air balloon, reaching the height of 11,400 ft (3500 m), did not have the necessary funding to construct his new balloon. Finally, the French government and Jeffries decided to finance Pilâtre, so he could build his balloon capable of crossing the English Channel in the opposite direction and against the prevailing winds.

48-49 THE BALLOON OF
ABBOT MIOLAN AND THE
ENGRAVER JANINET SHOULD
HAVE TAKEN OFF ON SUNDAY
JULY 11TH, 1784 AT EXACTLY
MIDDAY FROM THE JARDIN DE
LUXEMBOURG, IN PARIS.
HOWEVER, FOR UNKNOWN
REASONS, THE BALLOON
CAUGHT FIRE. FROM THAT
POINT ON THE POOR
PHYSICISTS WERE DERIDED
MERCILESSLY BY ALL MANNER
OF SONGS AND CARICATURES
AT ALL THE STALLS OF THE FAIR.

49 THE DEATH OF FRENCH
BALLOONIST JEAN-FRANÇOIS
PILÂTRE DE ROZIER AND HIS
ASSISTANT PIERRE-ANGEL
ROMAIN WHEN THEIR
BALLOON BURST INTO
FLAMES WHILE THEY WERE
ATTEMPTING TO CROSS THE
ENGLISH CHANNEL ON JUNE
15TH, 1785.

Pilâtre's design was advanced for its time and was both a hydrogen and a hot air balloon. This was a completely new concept which combined a sphere-shaped upper part, filled with hydrogen, and a cylinder in the lower part, which acted as a hot air balloon. However, it was difficult to be controlled by means of the steering devices available. Two centuries later, the fans of the modern hot air balloon would call this type of aerostat a Rozière Balloon, in honor of its inventor. Despite the advice of Etienne Montgolfier, who considered it too dangerous, Pilâtre and his assistant Pierre Romain took-off from Boulogne on June 15, 1785. After few minutes the balloon exploded and caught fire and crashed to the ground not far away from Wimereux. Both men were killed. Pilâtre, the first man to fly, became the first to die in an aircraft crash. The tragedy of Pilâtre marked the end of hot air balloons, which would only make a reappearance in the 1960s.

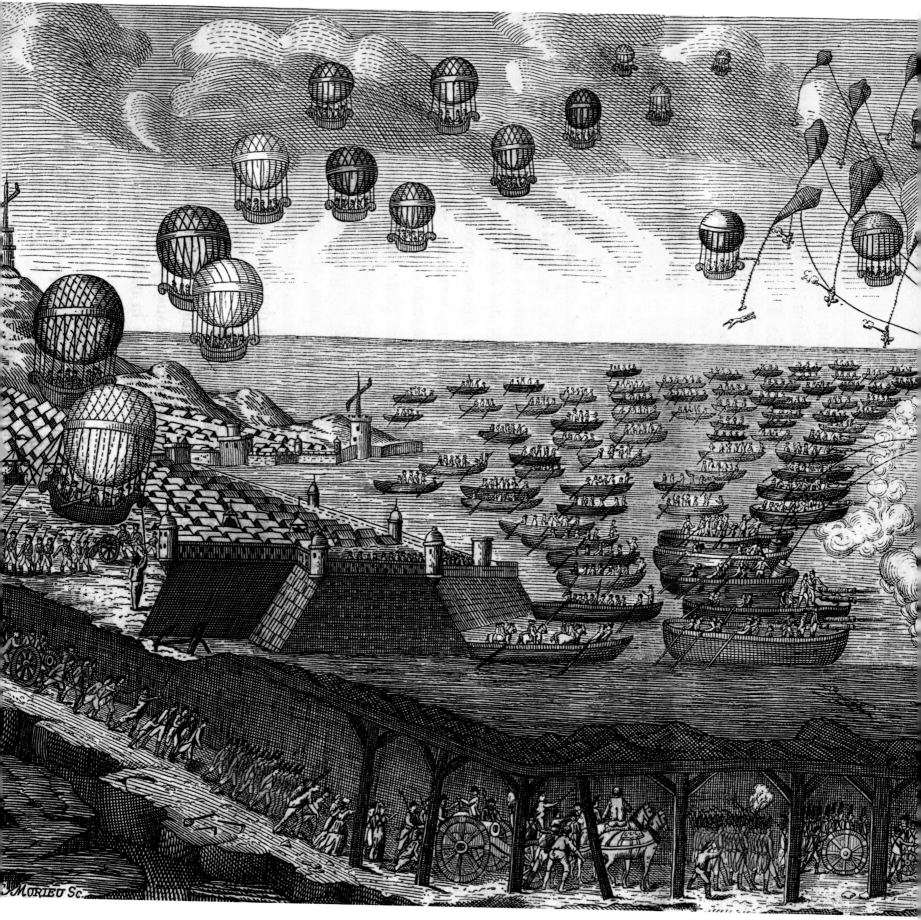

J.MORIEU Sc.

THE "BALLOON MANIA"

The "balloon mania" of 1783 developed almost overnight after the first successes of the hot air and gas balloon flights in France, or perhaps it woulbe be better called a "flight mania."

The great interest in these first flights had an impact not only on science, but also art and everyday life. It was something that fascinated every social class, from the poorest to the richest. The ladies at court wore their hair in styles called "Montgolfier" or "flying globe," "Blanchard," or even "inflammable air." There were flashy clothes, with swellings on skirts and on the puffed sleeves

of the dresses, and men's fashion, too, was influenced by the ballooning craze. The spread of "balloon mania" was extraordinary. Many majolica factories launched tableware designs called *au balloon*. Moustiers was the most famous factory to produce objects of every kind. Moustiers, in contrast to the faience factories of Sèvres and the other maiolica producers of Strasbourg, were greatly inspired by the exploits of Charles and Robert. They produced salad bowls, shaving plates (often with inscriptions such as "Have a nice journey"), and *au ballon* maiolicas which com-

50-51 IN 1806 NAPOLEON WAS PRESENTED WITH THE IDEA OF A BALLOON EXPEDITION WITH SOLDIERS ON BOARD. TAKING ADVANTAGE OF THE FIRST FAVORABLE WIND, THEY WOULD HAVE CHALLENGED THE ENEMY FLEET BY FLYING OVER IT AND WOULD HAVE LANDED IN ENGLAND IN ONLY A FEW HOURS. ALTHOUGH THE PLAN WAS EVENTUALLY JUDGED TO BE UNFEASIBLE AND WAS ABANDONED, NAPOLEON WAS ALMOST CONVINCED TO AGREE TO THIS "MADNESS."

51 THE PLAN TO TRANSPORT AN ENTIRE ARMY BY BALLOON, DEVELOPED DURING THE SECOND HALF OF THE 18TH CENTURY, WAS NEVER PUT INTO PRACTICE.

memorated a particular flight. In Paris, an "air cream" was produced which was a kind of liqueur with a fine engraving of a balloonist on the label. From the end of 1786 the balloon flights did not fulfill the expectations of the popular imagination and the the mania progressively faded away.

The passion was reborn, however, in the 19th century thanks to the balloon festivals and the various flights for scientific purposes.

All these objects, inspired by the aerostatic balloon, remind further to the great discovery of the "lighter than air."

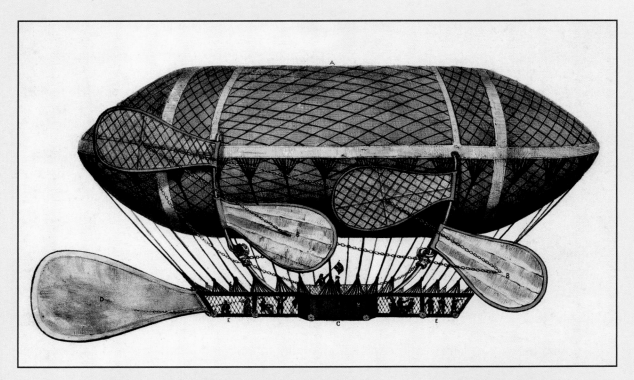

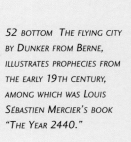

52 TOP "L'AIGLE," THE AIRSHIP BUILT BY THE COUNT OF LENNOX IN 1834 TO CREATE A DIRECT LINK BETWEEN THE VARIOUS EUROPEAN CAPITALS. THE FIRST AIRCRAFT OF THIS TYPE WAS DISPLAYED IN THE PARK OF THE ROYAL AERONAUTICAL SOCIETY IN KENSINGTON, LONDON. IT MEASURED ALMOST 50 METERS IN LENGTH, 15 METERS IN HEIGHT AND 12 METERS IN WIDTH AND HAD A VOLUME OF ALMOST 3000 CUBIC METERS. THE AIRCRAFT WAS CYLINDRICAL WITH CONICAL EXTREMITIES AND EIGHT PADDLE-SHAPED FLAPS, FOUR ON EACH SIDE, TO MOVE THE AIRCRAFT FORWARD OR BACKWARDS. THE AIRSHIP PROVED TO BE TOO HEAVY TO RISE AND WAS DESTROYED BY SPECTATORS AFTER A FAILED TAKE-OFF FROM THE CHAMPS DE MARS, ON AUGUST 17TH, 1834.

52 BOTTOM THE FLYING CITY BY DUNKER FROM BERNE, ILLUSTRATES PROPHECIES FROM THE EARLY 19TH CENTURY, AMONG WHICH WAS LOUIS SÉBASTIEN MERCIER'S BOOK "THE YEAR 2440."

53 THE TRUE ORIGINALITY OF BLANCHARD'S CREATION INCLUDED THE USE OF HYDROGEN AS FUEL AND THE UNPRECEDENTED USE OF A PROPELLER. JEAN-PIERRE BLANCHARD, A FRENCH ENGINEER, WAS THE FIRST TO HAVE THE IDEA OF USING PROPELLERS ATTACHED TO AIRBORNE ENGINES TO STEER A BALLOON, WHICH HE PREFERRED TO HAVE UNTETHERED. IN SHORT, HE INVENTED THE AIRSHIP. THE BLANCHARD AIRSHIP OF 1785 WAS FITTED WITH SAILS BUT IT NEVER WENT BEYOND THE PLANNING STAGE.

54 TOP AROUND 1784
"BALLOON HATS" BECAME
EXTREMELY FASHIONABLE
AMONG LADIES OF THE COURT
AS DID CLOTHING "EN DEMI-
BALLON" AND HAIR STYLED "À
LA BLANCHARD."

54 BOTTOM THE ENGRAVING
DEPICTS FLIGHTS OF FANTASY;
AROUND 1784 FASHION WAS
DOMINATED BY BALLOONS AND
ARTISTS LET THEIR IMAGINATION
RUN WILD IN THEIR PICTURES.
THE FASHION WAS CALLED
"BALLOONMANIA" AND IT
LASTED TEN YEARS. IN THIS
PICTURE, MEN AND WOMEN
TAKE OFF FROM THE WINDOWS
OF BUILDINGS SUPPORTED BY
UMBRELLAS AND BUTTERFLIES,
AS IF THEY HAD PARACHUTES.

55 FANTASY OF A BICYCLE
RIDE FROM THE EARTH TO THE
MOON. A MAN SCRUTINIZES
SPACE WITH A TELESCOPE AS HE
PEDALS ON A FLYING MACHINE
SIMILAR TO A BICYCLE WITH
WHEELS LIKE PROPELLERS,
SUSPENDED FROM TWO
BALLOONS. THIS ILLUSTRATION
IS TAKEN FROM A FRENCH
CARTOON "LE VOYAGE À LA
LUNE."

56 FANTASY OF A BICYCLE RIDE
FROM THE EARTH TO THE MOON.
A MAN SCRUTINIZES SPACE WITH
A TELESCOPE AS HE PEDALS ON
A FLYING MACHINE SIMILAR TO
A BICYCLE WITH WHEELS LIKE
PROPELLERS, SUSPENDED FROM
TWO BALLOONS. THIS
ILLUSTRATION IS TAKEN FROM A
FRENCH CARTOON "LE VOYAGE
À LA LUNE."

57 On the occasion of the Universal Exhibition in 1878 in Paris, Henri Giffard built a tethered balloon of 25,000 cubic meters, which could carry 40 to 50 passengers 500 meters above the ground. This became one of the major attractions, hence the poster advertising the "Russian Exhibition."

58 1871 CALENDAR WITH A PANORAMA OF PARIS FEATURING A GAS BALLOON FLYING OVERHEAD. THIS ENGRAVING DEPICTS A VIEW OF THE LOUVRE AND THE TUILERIES DURING THE SIEGE OF PARIS IN 1871, DURING WHICH BALLOONS WERE USED TO COMMUNICATE WITH AREAS OUTSIDE THE CITY.

58-59 THE SO-CALLED "NOUVEAU JEU DES BALLONS AÉROSTATIQUES À L'USAGE DES ESPRITS ÉLEVÉS," THE BALLOON GAME WITH ILLUSTRATIONS OF VARIOUS HOT-AIR BALLOONS FROM 1783 AND 1784.

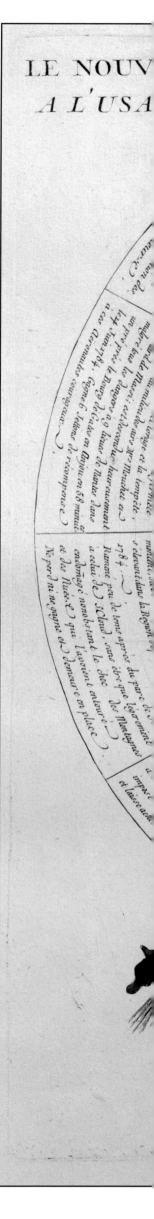

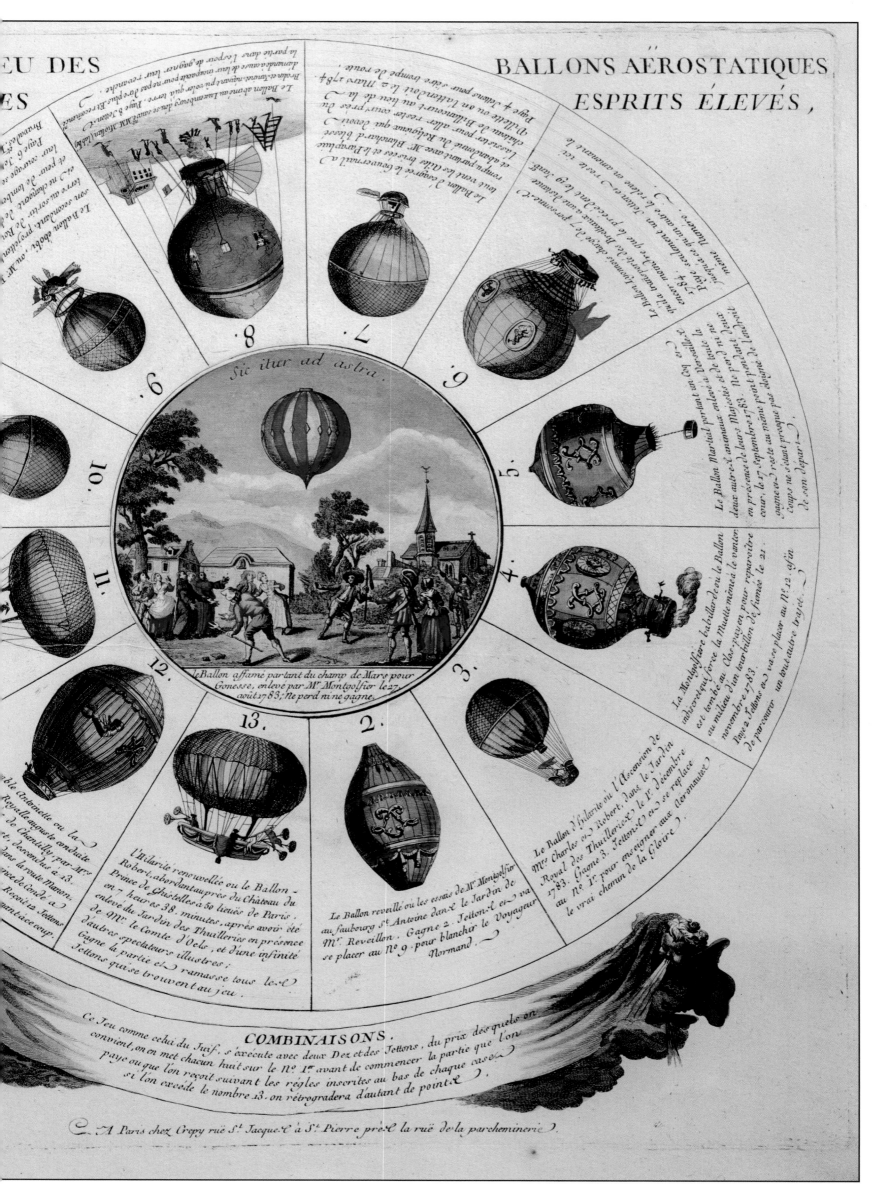

60-61 and 61 The departure of the great French statesman Léon Gambetta, on October 7th, 1870 on board the "Armand-Barbes" balloon during the siege of Paris. The picture on the right was an illustration from the front page of the French newspaper "L'illustration."

The interest in hot air balloons did not fade, as some people foretold, with the end of the 19th century, especially as gas balloons were preferred by most pilots at this time. However, at the beginning of the 20th century once again it was possible to see hot air balloons moving through the skies. In the 1960s this "new," or re-discovered, sport experienced a boom. The trend for ballooning came from the United States, where the Americans had created new fabrics, especially new nylons (already used for making spinnaker sails), new burners, which used liquid propane to warm up the envelope, and propane fuel tanks made of aluminum – a very light metal. Only the basket was still made of steel. All these developments made ballooning considerably safer. It was during this period that the design of the envelopes changed radically, with the use of all sorts of wonderful colors and patterns.

62 Gas balloons take off
on the occasion of the
first Balloon Festival in
Milan. The illustration was
published in "La Domenica
del Corriere" in 1904.

63 In May 1928, again in
Milan, a photographer from
the magazine "La Domenica
del Corriere" uses a hot air
balloon to take aerial
photographs.

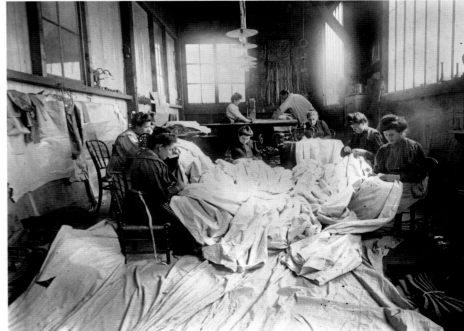

66 AND 67 THE SPENCER FAMILY WERE PIONEERS IN THE
MANUFACTURE OF AIRSHIPS IN ENGLAND. ENA SPENCER, THE ONLY
SURVIVING MEMBER OF THE ORIGINAL FAMILY, FOUGHT TO KEEP
SPENCER BROTHERS LTD. AS A FAMILY CONCERN. ON THE RIGHT, A
GROUP OF WORKERS TRANSPORTS A LARGE BALLOON, WHICH THEY HAVE
MADE, TO THE NEWINGTON PLANT, AGAIN MANAGED BY ENA SPENCER.

68-69 *Various gas balloons photographed before their departure on the day of the inauguration of the Aeronautical Park at the International Exhibition in Milan in 1906.*

TAKING THE
SKY BY STORM

70-71 *The fabric of Auguste Piccard's stratospheric balloon started to crack: the envelope had become too porous and could no longer be used as originally intended. After an attempt to convert it into a hot air balloon, it caught fire on May 25th, 1937 while flying over Belgium.*

*70 BOTTOM AUGUSTE
PICCARD AND PAUL KIPFER
MADE THE FIRST STRATOSPHERIC
FLIGHT DEPARTING FROM
AUGSBURG ON MAY 27TH,
1931. THEY REACHED AN
ALTITUDE OF 15,781 METERS.*

*71 PROFESSOR AUGUSTE
PICCARD (RIGHT) AND HIS
ASSISTANT PAUL KIPFER (LEFT)
SHOW OFF THEIR STEEL
"HELMETS," WHICH WERE TO
PROTECT THEM FROM HEAD
INJURIES AS THEIR CABIN
RE-ENTERED THE ATMOSPHERE.*

Since the beginning, aerostatics have fascinated man, and from the moment of their invention, man has attempted to create and break new records – height, distance, duration, great crossings and travel around the world – by taking advantage of the more recent research in various fields. Nearly everything has been tested, from the smallest to the biggest balloons. The most famous names descend directly from Pilâtre de Rozier, especially as they all use his exact invention, namely the Rozière balloon — Bertrand Piccard and Brian Jones have left their marks in the history of aerostatics by completing the first journey around the world without any stops.

In fact, before Bertrand Piccard, it was his grandfather, professor Auguste Piccard, who ascended as the first person in the stratosphere onboard a gas balloon. On 27 May 1931, in a pressurized cabin, the Swiss professor, accompanied by the engineer Paul Kipfer, reached an altitude of 51,775 ft (15,781 m) with a hydrogen balloon. This record was broken on 18 August 1932, when Auguste Piccard, accompanied by his Belgian colleague Max Cosyns, reached an altitude of 54,157 ft (16,507 m), for the first time detecting cosmic and gamma rays. They had taken off at 5 a.m. from Dübendorf airport (near Zurich) and at 5 p.m. landed in Italy, on the south side of Lake Garda, in the vicinity of Volta Mantovana. They had utilized a limp balloon, having a variable volume, with a cotton envelope coated with a rubber-based paint, able to dilate up to a volume of 494,405 cu ft (14,000 cu m), however, whilst ascending, the upper part had been inflated with only 98,881 cu ft (2800 cu m) of hydrogen.

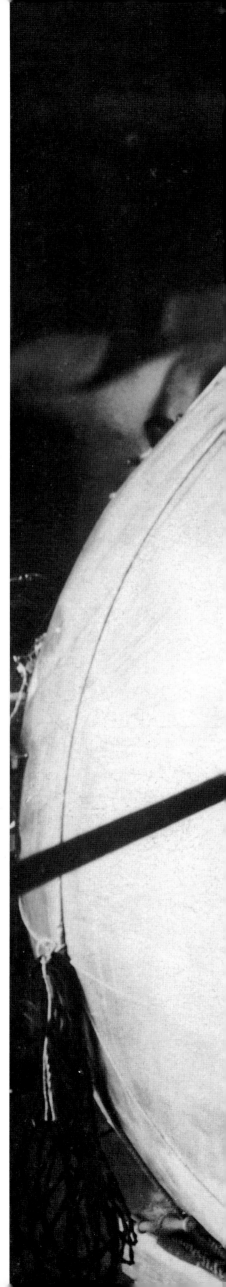

72 Swiss professor of Physics, Auguste Piccard, cuts his birthday cake in the shape of a stratospheric balloon, at the Hôtel de la Rue Moritz in New York. In 1932 Piccard reached the stratosphere at an altitude of 16,507 meters, establishing a new world record.

72-73 Auguste Piccard poses for photographers in the gondola of his stratospheric balloon, with which he reached an altitude of 16,000 meters in 1932.

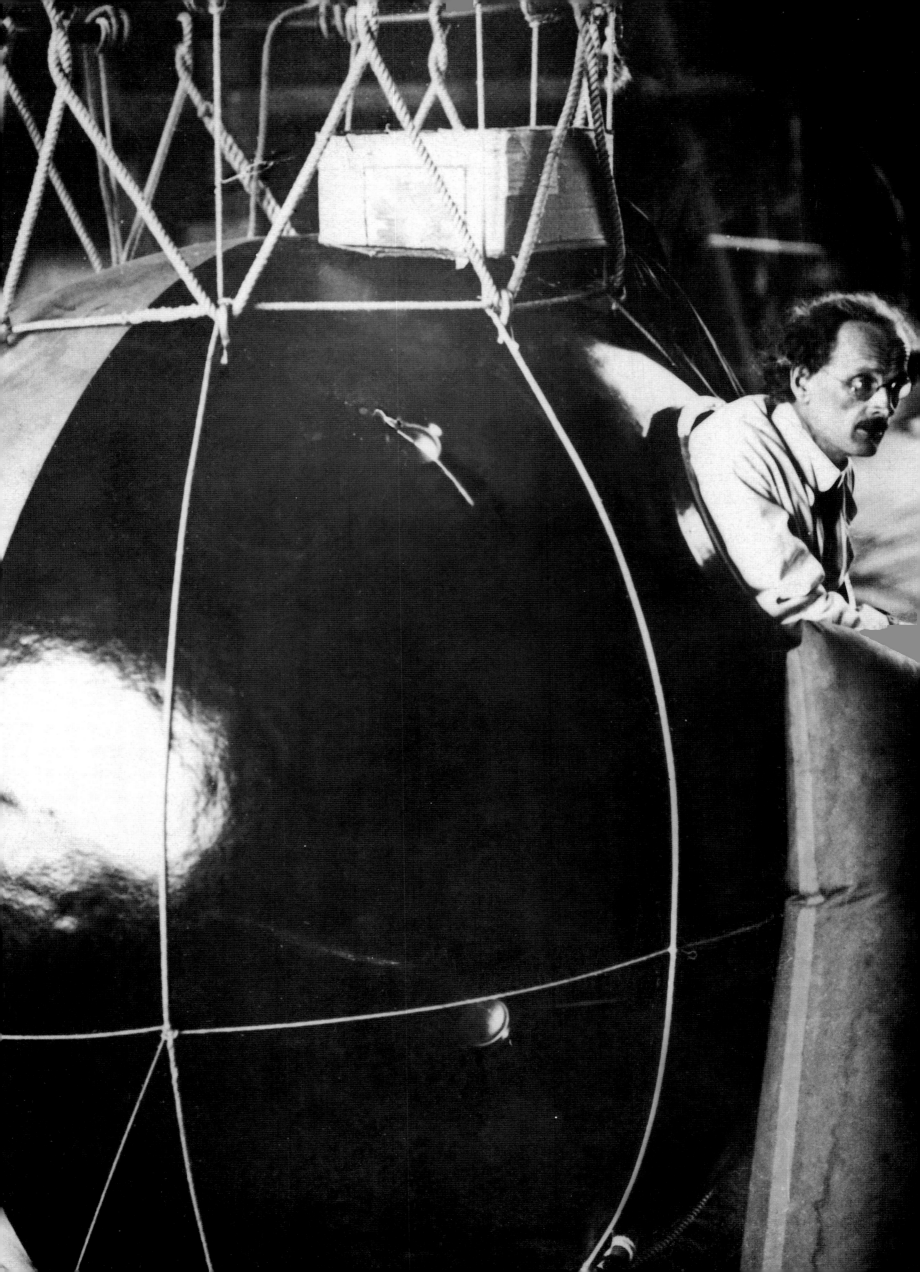

74-75 The new cabin of the balloon with which Auguste Piccard wanted to reach an altitude of 16,000 meters in 1932, is transported by truck. The cabin came from Belgium, passing through Zurich.

75 The National Foundation for Scientific Research accepted Professor Piccard's new program and so the balloon was to bear the "FNRS" initials of the institute. This time Piccard's flight companion was Max Cosyns, a young Belgian physicist. The two scientists were able to use the envelope from the previous flight but with a new gondola. Because of the winds, they decided to take off from the aerodrome in Dübendorf, near Zurich, in Switzerland. The area is natural basin surrounded by mountains and therefore sheltered from strong winds.

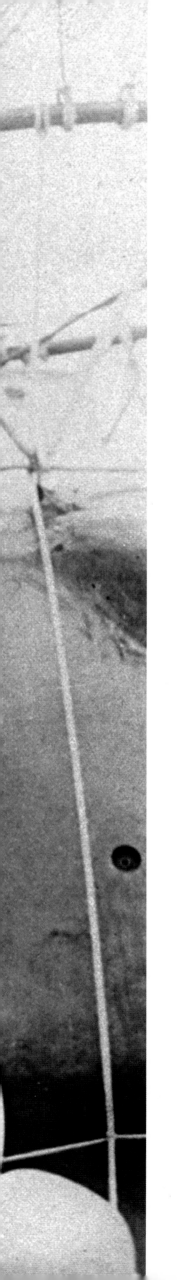

ILLUSTRAZIONE DEL POPOLO

Domenica 14 giugno 1931 (IX).   Supplemento della "GAZZETTA DEL POPOLO"   Anno XI - Numero 24

L'ascensione del prof. Piccard. — Dopo essere rimasto per molte ore nella stratosfera, ad un'altezza non mai raggiunta dall'uomo, il pallone dell'audace scienziato è disceso sul ghiacciaio del Gurgler, nelle Alpi tirolesi, dove la navicella sferica dell'aerostato rimarrà a ricordo della memorabile impresa.

(Disegno di Aldo Molinari).

In questo numero: Confidenze di Virgilio Brocchi

Le Petit Journal ILLUSTRÉ

HEBDOMADAIRE - 42ᵉ Année   7 Juin 1931 - Nᵒ 2111
61, rue Lafayette, Paris   PRIX : 50 CENTIMES

LE MAGNIFIQUE EXPLOIT DU PROFESSEUR PICCARD

77 AUGUSTE PICCARD'S ACHIEVEMENT AND HIS ALTITUDE RECORD WERE ON THE FRONT PAGES OF ALL THE MAGAZINES AND NEWSPAPERS. THE ITALIAN NEWSPAPER "ILLUSTRAZIONE DEL POPOLO" (TOP) AND THE SWISS "PETIT JOURNAL ILLUSTRÉ" (BOTTOM), WHICH SHOWS AUGUSTE PICCARD'S BALLOON LANDING ON A GLACIER.

In September 1933, the Russians Prokofief, Birnbaum and Godunov reached an altitude of 56,443 ft (17,204 m) and, in November 1933, the military balloon Century of Progress broke this record again by touching an altitude of 61,237 ft (18,665 m). In 1935 two captains of the American Army, Orvil Anderson and Albert William Stevens, attained an altitude of 72,441 ft (22,080 m).

In the years prior to the Second World War there was a period of great development in the use of dirigibles, especially Germany's Zeppelins. March 4, 1936 saw the first flight of the Zeppelin LZ 129 Hindenburg, which was the biggest and most luxurious dirigible that had ever been constructed. Initially, it was designed to be inflated with helium, which had to be delivered from the USA. However, because of the American trade embargo the helium was replaced with hydrogen, which is an inflammable gas. On May 6, 1937 the Hindenburg exploded as it came into dock at the city of Lakehurst in the USA: 35 passengers died and 54 survived.

78 THE TWO AMERICAN ARMY CAPTAINS , ALBERT WILLIAMS STEVENS AND ORVIL ANDERSON, PREPARE FOR A STRATOSPHERIC FLIGHT AND POSE IN FRONT OF THE GONDOLA OF "EXPLORER II."

78-79 "EXPLORER II" LANDING ON THE PLAINS NEAR WHITE LAKE, SOUTH DAKOTA, AFTER A STRATOSPHERIC FLIGHT THAT REACHED AN ALTITUDE OF 22,080 METERS ON NOVEMBER 11 TH, 1935.

LIFE

RICHARD M. NIXON
WRITES ABOUT
NATIONAL PURPOSE

RECORD JUMP STARTS
NINETEEN MILES UP

AUGUST 29, 1960

In the course of the investigation into the disaster it was suggested that the most plausible cause was sabotage in order to discredit the Nazis. However, the dirigibles that used hydrogen were highly inflammable and always risked exploding. The fire could have been caused by static electricity accumulated due to the thunderous weather conditions, or by a malfunction of the electric circuits or of the engines.

The altitude record would not be broken until 1960 when new balloons with polyethylene envelopes, utilizing helium as the inflation gas were used. On 27 August 1960, the American Joe Kittinger ascended to 102,798 ft (31,333 m) in 1 hour and 31 minutes: then he launched himself in the emptiness. His freefall ended at 18,045 ft (5500 m), when his parachute opened automatically. This record has not been approved because the pilot was not onboard the aerostat at the moment of landing, however, the undertaking has been recorded.

On 4 May 1961, the biggest aerostat ever piloted, a helium balloon of 10,099,995 cu ft (286,000 cu m), — the Strato-lab High 5 of the US Navy — carried two Americans, Malcolm Ross and Victor Prather to an altitude of 113,740 ft (34,668 m) in 2 hours and 39 minutes.

And hot air balloons? It was Indian Dr. Vijaypat Singhania, who achieved an altitude record of 68,898 ft (21,000 m), on 25 November 2005. He took off from the city center of Mumbai, India, onboard a hot-air balloon model Z-1600 with a volume of 1,589,160 cu ft (45,000 cu m), constructed by Cameron Balloons. It had a pressurized basket, built by Andy Elson and the engineering team The Flying Pictures, with a total weight of 3,968 lb (1,800 kg). The previous altitude record for a hot air balloon of 64,997 ft (19,811 m), had been achieved by the Swede Per Lindstrand in Plano, Texas, in June 1988.

80 THE COVER OF THE AMERICAN "LIFE" MAGAZINE DISPLAYED A PHOTO OF JOSPEH KITTINGER, AN OFFICER IN THE UNITED STATES AIR FORCE, IN A 25,800-METER FREE FALL. THE CLOUDS UNDERNEATH HIM ARE AT A DISTANCE OF 24 KILOMETERS. JOSEPH KITTINGER JUMPED FROM AN ALTITUDE OF 31,333 METERS. THIS RECORD DATES BACK TO AUGUST 16TH, 1960. THE CAPTAIN (RIGHT) IS WEARING A SPECIAL SUIT FOR THIS STRATOSPHERE JUMP.

81 JOSEPH KITTINGER BROKE HIS OWN RECORD FROM THE GONDOLA OF "EXCELSIOR III" OVER NEW MEXICO. THE FALL LASTED 4 MINUTES AND 36 SECONDS, AT A SPEED OF 1000 KM/H. KITTINGER OPENED HIS PARACHUTE AT 5500 METERS, ESTABLISHING TWO RECORDS THAT REMAIN UNBROKEN.

AS FAR AS POSSIBLE

A further challenge, with which aeronauts have faced themselves, is to travel as far as possible aboard their aerostats, and this includes both hot air balloons and gas balloons. These long flights, which utilize more modern techniques, have allowed the first crossings of the Atlantic Ocean.

The year 1978 marked the history of the Atlantic crossing of the Double Eagle II. On 30 July 1978, Don Cameron and Chris Davey attempted the undertaking onboard a Rozière balloon, but they failed at only 115 miles (185 km) from the Breton coast — the ultimate misfortune, because 20 days later three Americans succeeded in this venture. Ben Abruzzo, Maxie Anderson and Larry Newman took off from Presque Isle, in Maine. It was their second attempt, having failed in the sea of Ireland a year earlier. However, this was a successful undertaking, and after 137 hours and 6 minutes, the Double Eagle II, which contained 160,081 cu ft (4,533 cu m) of helium and measured 96.7 ft (29.5 m) in height and 65 ft (19.8 m) in width, landed in France in the vicinity of Evreux, 61 miles from Paris. The loading capacity of the balloon for the ascent was 10,509 lb (4,767 kg), of which 6,246 lb (2,833 kg) was ballast.

Joe Kittinger also wished to leave his mark in the history books so he attempted the crossing onboard his helium balloon Rosie O'Grady, between 14 and 18 September 1984. He took off alone from Caribou in Maine and arrived in Italy 83 hours and 40 minutes later, passing over 3,534 miles (5,688 km). Christophe Houver and Laurent Lajoye were the first two French pilots who crossed the Atlantic onboard

a Rozière balloon of 7,692 cu ft (2,200 cu m). They ascended from Saint-John, in Canada, on 30 August 2000, and landed in Sion, in Normandy, France on 5 September, flying at a maximum altitude of 17,119 ft (5,218 m).

However, all these crossings sowed a seed in Don Cameron's mind, and he conceived the idea of a new competition: The Atlantic Crossing. The balloon manufacturer decided to organize the race for 1992. All the competitors had the same type of aerostat — the Rozière Cameron R-77 class AM-8 — equipped with identical burners, called stealth burners. In this way the competitors would utilize materials with identical characteristics.

82 TOP ON AUGUST 11TH, 1978 AN AMERICAN TEAM ATTEMPTED THE FIRST ATLANTIC CROSSING ON BOARD THE "DOUBLE EAGLE II" BALLOON, SEEN HERE IN FRONT OF A "T8" ROYAL AIR FORCE RECONNAISSANCE PLANE. THE BALLOON CREW WAS MADE UP OF LARRY NEWMAN, MAX ANDERSON, AND BEN ABRUZZO.

82 BOTTOM FINALLY, ON AUGUST 17TH, 1978, THE THREE AMERICAN PILOTS COMPLETE THE ATLANTIC BALLOON CROSSING, WHICH TOOK MORE THAN FIVE DAYS. FIFTY YEARS AFTER LINDBERGH'S FLIGHT, THE CREW ARRIVED IN PARIS. FROM LEFT: BEN ABRUZZO, MAXIE ANDERSON, AND LARRY NEWMAN.

83 THE FAMOUS BALLOON PILOT, JOE KITTINGER, A RETIRED US AIR FORCE COLONEL, MAKES THE FINAL ADJUSTMENTS TO THE LOAD RING OF HIS BALLOON "ROSIE O'GRADY'S FLYING CIRCUS."

84 TOP BERTRAND PICCARD, AUGUSTE PICCARD'S GRANDSON, MAKES HIS DÉBUT IN THE WORLD OF BALLOONS ON THE OCCASION OF THE FIRST TRANSATLANTIC RACE IN 1992. HERE, ON BOARD THE GONDOLA, BERTRAND PICCARD WRITES ABOUT HIS ADVENTURE IN HIS LOGBOOK AS THE BALLOON FLIES OVER THE OCEAN.

84 BOTTOM THE TAKE OFF OF THE FIRST BALLOON FOR THE TRANSATLANTIC

COMPETITION, FOUNDED BY THE FAMOUS AEROSTATIC BALLOON PRODUCER DON CAMERON AND HIS ENGINEER ALAN NOBLE, ON THE NIGHT OF 15TH SEPTEMBER 1992. THE "CHRYSLER TRANSATLANTIC CHALLENGE" PUT BALLOON PILOTS FROM ALL OVER THE WORLD TO THE TEST. THE CREWS HAD TO LAND IN EUROPE, EXCLUDING IRISH TERRITORY. THE TEAM WHICH CROSSED THE ATLANTIC IN THE SHORTEST TIME WON.

84-85 *ALL THE GONDOLAS TAKING PART IN THE "CHRYSLER TRANSATLANTIC CHALLENGE" WERE IDENTICAL. IN THE PHOTOGRAPH, THE BALLOON OF THE BERTRAND PICCARD FROM SWITZERLAND AND THE BELGIAN VIM VERSTRAETEN, THE WINNER OF THE COMPETITION.*

For this first race to cross the Atlantic, called the Chrysler Transatlantic Challenge, there were five teams. The five balloons took off on September 16, 1992, from Bangor, Maine. The balloon piloted by Swiss Bertrand Piccard and the Belgian Vim Verstraeten was the first to make the crossing, reaching Spain after a flight of 122 hours. Naturally, Don Cameron, founder of the race, participated and was accompanied by Rob Bayly. They reached the Portuguese coast. The race was a great success, however, unfortunately, for the moment it has not been repeated. Nevertheless, Don Cameron has not lost his hope to organize another challenge in the near future. In the same year, Don Cameron also took off from London in the Rozière R-77, which was identical to the balloons used in the Chrysler Transatlantic Challenge, and landed close to St. Petersburg. The ultimate dream of every pilot is to be the first person to fly a balloon around the world. A new race was launched using the revolutionary Rozières, called after Pilâtre de Rozier, the first pilot who designed the original prototype in the eighteenth century. It was on board his new invention, which he had called an "aero-montgolfier," on June 15, 1785 that Pilâtre de Rozier died during his attempt to cross the English Channel.

AROUND THE WORLD ONBOARD A BALLOON

A new challenge awaited the adventurers of the sky: the conquest of the title to be the first human being to completely transverse the globe without any stops, utilizing only the jet streams. These streams develop at the limits of the tropopause, at about 32,800 ft (10,000 m) in altitude, and they can push the balloon at high speeds exceeding 125 mph (200 km/h). This is not a real race, but a serious challenge, into which

The Virgin owner had technician Per Lindstrand and his former rival, American Steve Fossett as his co-crew members. For Fossett this was his fifth attempt in four years.

As the most experienced of the pilots, Steve Fossett had excited pilots in August 1998 when, on his fourth attempt ascending from Mendoza, Argentina, the American millionaire had crashed into the Pacific after a violent thunderstorm; he

many teams have launched themselves in order to establish the record and leave behind a mark in the history of aeronautics.

1999 was a decisive year, and it marked the first attempts to circumnavigate the world. One year after a season characterized by calamities and failures, six aeronautic crews prepared to start the adventure and to use their fragile devices in an attempt to travel around the world onboard a balloon for the first time in the history of aviation.

The British millionaire Richard Branson was the first pilot who announced his intention to take off from Marrakech, in Morocco, for his third attempt to travel across the world on a balloon.

had completed two thirds of the route. The dream had never seemed so accessible.

Their adversary, Bertrand Piccard, got on board for his third and last attempt with his Breitling Orbiter together with the Britain Brian Jones.

If up until this point the Swiss had realized the longest flight, then Kevin Uliassi instead had concluded the shortest. He took off on 31 December from Loves Park, in Illinois, and three hours later the American landed his basket in the nearby state of Indiana. The balloon was perforated! At the age of 35 years, he was the only one who tried again to perform this tour alone.

86 STEVE FOSSETT (RIGHT) WITH RICHARD BRANSON (CENTER) AND PER LINDSTRAND (LEFT) IN THE DESERT NEAR MARRAKECH IN MOROCCO, ON THE EVE OF THEIR TAKE OFF FOR A ROUND-THE-WORLD JOURNEY BY BALLOON.

86-87 DECEMBER 17TH, 1998, THE HELIUM BALLOON IS INFLATED IN THE MARRAKECH DESERT IN MOROCCO, ON THE EVE OF THE DEPARTURE OF STEVE FOSSETT, RICHARD BRANSON, AND PER LINDSTRAND FOR THEIR ROUND-THE-WORLD JOURNEY.

87 TOP THE HELICOPTERS OF THE HAWAII COAST GUARD AFTER RESCUING FOSSET, BRANSON AND LINDSTRAND, WHO FAILED IN THEIR ROUND-THE-WORLD BY BALLOON ATTEMPT ON DECEMBER 25TH, 1998.

The Britain Andy Elson, who had been a part-
ner in the misfortune of Piccard in February, took
off in the winter of 1999 together with his com-
patriot Colin Prescot. Their balloon Cable and
Wireless was supposed to accelerate its speed by
using kerosene and not propane like the others.
The departure was planned to start from Almeria,
Spain.

In order combat all these "recidivists", the
American-Australian trio Dave Liniger, Bob Martin
and John Wallington wanted an audacious ap-
proach. In 1997 this trio had remained on the
ground due to lack of money, but their Re/Max

ascended from Australia for the circumnavigation to ... 118 ft (36 m) in altitude!

As regards the last crew participating in this race, an American-British trio champed at the bit in Albuquerque, New Mexico. Their Spirit of Peace would be, according to them, the first balloon to realize this "last great *première*." The die was cast, who would win? All the participants studied each other and examined the weather forecasts. The coming months would be crucial in order to realize this historical flight.

The first ascension was performed by the IC-CO Global Challenge, with Richard Branson, and

the adventure was concluded at Christmas in the Pacific, in the region of Honolulu.

On 15 January team Re/Max gave up their dream of traveling around the world, after being grounded for 20 days due to bad meteorological conditions.

On 17 February, it was the turn of Britain's Colin Prescot and Andy Elson who, in a new attempt to make a tour around the world, took off from Almeria, in southern Spain, onboard the Cable and Wireless balloon, while Bertrand Piccard, with the Breitling Orbiter III waited in Château-d'Oex for favorable weather conditions.

88 BOTTOM ON OCTOBER 29TH, 1998 TWO BRITONS, COLIN PRESCOTT AND ANDY ELSON, (RIGHT) CHOSE THE NAME "CABLE AND WIRELESS" FOR THE CAPSULE OF THEIR NEW BALLOON, WITH WHICH THEY WOULD ATTEMPT TO COMPLETE THE ROUND-THE-WORLD TRIP.

88-89 PILOTS COLIN PRESCOTT AND ANDY ELSON (RIGHT) INSIDE THEIR CAPSULE. THE TWO BRITONS STAYED ON BOARD THEIR "CABLE AND WIRELESS" BALLOON FOR 17 DAYS AND 18 HOURS BEFORE THEY WERE FORCED TO SPLASH DOWN OFF THE JAPANESE COAST DUE TO BAD WEATHER CONDITIONS.

On Monday, 1 March, at 9.05 a.m., the Breitling Orbiter III took off from the small resort of Pays d'Enhaut, in Switzerland. The envelope of 180 ft (55 m) in height, which carried a basket of over 8 tons, ascended majestically towards France. Bertrand Piccard and Brian Jones launched themselves into the race in the Cable and Wireless, which had started on 17 February. The British crew, which had 12 days advantage on its pursuers, could not, like Piccard, fly in the aisle running over China, and this caused delay over the Bengal Gulf. On 4 March, as Orbiter III flew over Mauritania and turned toward Egypt, Andy Elson and Colin Prescot left Vietnamese air space. On 6 March Bertrand Piccard, together with his British co-pilot, flew over the Red Sea and aimed

toward Mecca, in Saudi Arabia. They moved forward slowly and hoped to meet the powerful jet streams within the next 24 hours. In the meantime the Cable and Wireless was flying over the China Sea and preparing to enter into Japanese air space. However, the dream of the British aeronauts broke down on 7 March over the Pacific Ocean, in the region of Japan, after having actually achieved a new record for the duration of a flight without any intermediary stops.

In the previous hours, while they were flying over Japan and were traveling in a northerly direction, they had tried to catch the strong air currents to facilitate the Pacific crossing, but a low-pressure zone in the southeast of the archipelago had prevented the balloon from catching the right

air stream. In their last hours the crew tried to ascend over a cloud bank and to recharge their batteries, however, the current pushed them to far east and both men decided that it was necessary to make a stop.

At this moment the Piccard/Jones crew proceeded alone in an attempt to complete the trip around the world. On 8 March Orbiter III turned to India, and on 9 March it was already traveling toward Bangladesh at a speed of 65 mph (100 km/h) and at an altitude of 25,919 ft (7,900 m). After a flight time of eight days the crew had already passed 7,860 miles (12,650 km) since take off in Switzerland. By the evening the balloon was traveling toward China at a speed of 75 mph (120 km/h). On 10 March, strictly follow-

90-91 MONDAY, MARCH
1ST, 1999, BERTRAND
PICCARD PREPARES TO TAKE OFF
FROM CHÂTEAU-D'OEX, IN
SWITZERLAND, ON BOARD THE
"ORBITER III" FOR HIS THIRD
ATTEMPT TO CIRCUMNAVIGATE
THE EARTH BY BALLOON.

91 AT 9 A.M., ON MARCH
1ST, 1999 ,THE BALLOON OF
BERTRAND PICCARD AND BRIAN
JONES TAKES OFF FROM
CHÂTEAU D'OEX, A SMALL SKI
RESORT IN THE VAUD ALPS.

ing the corridor, and authorized by Peking, Orbiter III flew over the Yunnan province, in the southwest of China. Piccard's balloon had crossed China in only 14 days, coasting with the precision of a Swiss clockmaker in the 26° parallel, on the northern side where they were not authorized to fly. On the 11th day of their adventure, during the flight over the Marianne islands at a speed of 38 mph (60 km/h) and an altitude of 24,934 ft (7,600 m), Bertrand Piccard and Brian Jones had completed one-thirds of their long voyage. It was one of the most dangerous stages due to the storms and the ocean's immensity. On 12 March, the Breitling Orbiter III was traveling towards the subtropical jet stream and finally, on 15 March, they found the much-desired jet streams and

could fly to the Hawaii region at a higher speed. The odometer showed 16,155 miles (26,000 km): both aeronauts had broken the distance record belonging to the American Steve Fossett!

On 16 March, after 15 days of flight, the Breitling Orbiter III managed a perfect maneuver within the jet stream, and forging ahead at a speed of 112 mph (180 km/h) the balloon arrived in Mexico by the evening. On 18 March a great fright occurred when the flight of the Breitling Orbiter III risked collision with a current, which pushed the balloon in the direction of Venezuela. Fortunately, the swift reactions of the meteorologists and crew made it possible to re-orientate the balloon to the east. Only ascension to more than 36,089 ft (11,000 m) allowed them to put

the aerostat back on the right route, and they took off toward the African coast at 62 mph (110 km/h). In the morning of 19 March, after a flight of 17 days, 18 hours and 25 minutes, the duration record established by Andy Elson and Colin Prescott was broken: the balloon was flying over the Atlantic at a speed of 96 mph (155 mk/h).

On 20 March their attempt was successful; at 9.54 GMT the Breitling Orbiter III passed over Mauritania, 9.27 degrees Western longitude, which signaled the final target of the trip around the world. Bertrand Piccard and Brian Jones had crossed 26,600 miles (42,810 km) within 19 days, 1 hour and 49 minutes, and now they continued the route to Egypt.

On 21 March, at 6.03 GMT, the balloon touched down without accidents in the sand in the vicinity of Dakhla in Egypt, 495 miles (800 km) southwest from Cairo. They took 19 days 21 hours and 47 minutes to conclude this first trip around the world without stops onboard a balloon. A real undertaking! They had broken all records of duration and distance on a balloon (28,355 miles).

The Rozières, protagonist of great expeditions and records, can be considered a balloon powered by solar energy. This model combines the hot air balloon and the gas balloon principles: helium (the gas that has replaced hydrogen) is pumped into the envelope of a hot air balloon. Inflammable hydrogen was replaced by helium when, in 1978, Don Cameron attempted to cross the Atlantic for the first time. The gas contained in the balloon envelope di-

lates due to the heating effect, and in this way it improves the balloon power, however the gas contracts the balloon when temperatures fall. Therefore, classical gas balloons have to carry ballast (sand bags), which can be unhooked in the night, to slow down the descent of the aerostat. On a Rozière balloon, the burners maintain the optimum dilatation temperature of the gas during the night, which negates the need for ballast, and allows a smaller balloon to be used. During departure the envelope is filled with helium only to half of its volume and at the moment of ascension, the diminishing of the pressure and the warming up of the gas due to the effect of the sun, allows the helium to attain the cruising volume. The advantage of this combination is the lack of need for ballast to slow down the descent of the balloon in the cold of the night; now only burners

are used to stabilize the balloon — and only a minimal amount of propane is required to warm up the helium. A further advantage of this system is the possibility of further reduced dimensions in comparison with a hot air balloon loaded with tons of ballast. The Rozière was not but a solar balloon powered with helium (a harmless and inert gas, which contracts itself in the night due to the lower temperatures), closed in an envelope of a hor air balloon. On this way, the helium balloon is in the environment of hot air. The principle is simple: during the day the Rozière is warmed-up by the sun beams and, in order to avoid the regulation of the temperature by night, the pilot warms-up the hot air balloon by activating the burner. On this way the heat inside the envelope is constant, and the helium does not lose his physical characteristics.

92 The "Orbiter III" in the sky of Chateau-d'Oex, a few minutes after take-off in a new round-the-world attempt.

93 top After flying for almost 20 days, on March 21st, 1999 the balloon of Bertrand Piccard and Brian Jones landed in the Egyptian desert. This, the first non-stop round-the-world trip by the "Breitling Orbiter III," was also the longest flight, by time and distance (42,810 kilometers), in the history of aviation.

93 bottom The day after their landing in the Egyptian desert, Brian Jones (left) and Bertrand Piccard, winners of the round-the-world contest, arrive triumphant in Geneva.

THE BALLOONS OF TOMORROW

It was not until the beginning of the twentieth century, however, that we witnessed a rebirth of balloons, which had disappeared completely during the previous century. For many years airships had largely replaced hot-air balloons, and even the advent of the airplane did not halt the enthusiasm and development of airships, which had become increasingly reliable and fast. During the First World War, the Germans built 123 of them; there was room for 100 passengers on board and they crossed the Atlantic at an average speed of 100 km/h.

It was not until 1920 that any attempt was made to bring hot-air balloons back to their former glory. However, there was still the problem of the use of fuel. In 1937 Professor Piccard and an American, Hay Cosyn, invented a propane gas burner.

In 1947 Don Piccard, the twin brother of the famous Professor, Auguste Piccard, started flying again in gas balloons but he still had the problem of finding hydrogen.

A turning point was marked by the creation of much lighter synthetic fabrics, coated nylon (which was much more resistant) and the new, more efficient propane-powered burners.

American companies were the first to begin production. Raven produced an aerostat, the "Vulcoon," which in the '60s marked the beginning of modern balloon flights. Later Don Piccard (again) and his friend, the physics student Tracy Barns, who built his first balloon in 1961, organized a rally to present the new balloons. Barnes abandoned his studies and became a balloon producer.

Thanks to these technological transformations, balloons acquired a new appearance, and the technical evolution continued.

Within the context of this rebirth of balloons, one man deserves special mention. Don Cameron founded the first balloon factory in 1971 and in 1976 produced the first balloon in his own company, Cameron Balloons in Bristol, England.

Cameron turned a hobby into a job, so much so that he now owns a company that employs 80 people and produces a balloon every day.

So how could we not mention this man who, in the rebirth of modern balloons and in the aerostatic world, is as important as the Montgolfier brothers, inventors of the principle of hot-air balloons 200 years earlier?

Don Cameron was born in Glasgow and attended the Allan Glen School in the same city, proceeding to study at Glasgow University where he graduated in Aeronautical Engineering. Two years later Don obtained another degree in the United States and soon after joined the Bristol Airplane Company.

He had a great passion for aeronautics and everything connected with it – including adventure – and together with some friends he created an association that produced the first modern hot-air balloon in Western Europe; the "Bristol Belle." In 1992, with Tom Sage and Terry Adams, he made a flight on the occasion of the Bristol Rally.

It is to Don Cameron that we owe the initiative to use Velcro for the "parachute valves" of balloons. It was also he who introduced the double-fold with two-centimeter stitching, with each edge sewn into the fold of another panel. Only 20 years later he created a burner with a flexi-rigid support system, which was subsequently modified slightly. This burner is still used today.

But the ingenious Cameron did not stop there. He did not stop making new inventions to improve balloon flying, both in relation to the weight of the materials and also the technology of the products used. In 1980 he changed the polyurethane fabric for another softer and more resistant material. By the time Cameron Balloons Ltd. celebrated 21 years in business, Don had already produced 3000 balloons.

After flying around the world in 1999, Don stated in his typically British way, "That's it, there's nothing left to do ... but you always find things to do." Indeed, many improvements have been made to balloons, particularly in methods for deflating balloons, but the general public does not notice this.

In the summer of 2008, in his workshop in Bristol, Cameron produced a prototype of a gondola made of a composite fiberglass material. "I think that this is the future but people love tradition and baskets, " he said. "The good thing is that this basket is much lighter than wicker, but this is just the beginning."

Cameron said: "In the first race there were five balloons that were airborne for four to five days over the ocean. Today, it is possible to have direct communication during these four or five days. Television advertising would be marvelous … and above all it would be very effective for sponsors. It would be interesting for the general public to watch these balloon races in real time, and in addition, television companies should find that it is good business for them."

94 LEFT DON CAMERON, THE BALLOON MANUFACTURER WITH HEADQUARTERS IN BRISTOL, ENGLAND, CELEBRATES THE 40TH ANNIVERSARY OF HIS FIRST FLIGHT. CAMERON PRODUCED THE FIRST HOT AIR BALLOON, THE "BRISTOL BELLE," WHICH FLEW FOR THE FIRST TIME IN WESTON-ON-THE-GREEN IN OXFORDSHIRE ON JULY 9TH, 1967.

94 CENTER THE TR-60 IS A MODERN, ELONGATED RACING BALLOON THAT PERMITS RAPID DESCENT AND ASCENT.

94 RIGHT THE "CLOUD HOPPER" IS A ONE-SEATER BALLOON AND THE PILOT SITS ON THE PROPANE CYLINDER.

95 LEFT USING A LARGER ENVELOPE, THE "CLOUD HOPPER" CAN CARRY TWO PEOPLE, STILL WITHOUT A GONDOLA; THE SECOND SEAT IS SUSPENDED FROM THE BALLOON.

95 RIGHT BEFORE TAKING OFF, THE PILOT OF THE "CLOUD HOPPER" TESTS THE BURNER THAT IS FUELED BY TWO PROPANE CYLINDERS, ON THE GROUND.

"Future" also means finding new fabrics, but since the invention of nylon 50 years ago, there have been no other inventions. Cameron said, "We need to come up with a fabric that has better insulating properties in order to reduce the consumption of fuel, but we are also studying balloons that can be powered by solar energy. Using silver-aluminized fabrics for example." Cameron has ventured into a new idea of a balloon that can best be described as being in the sustainable development class. "A sort of 'green' balloon, that does not pollute and without any CO2 emissions. A solar balloon that could have two different layers of fabric."

By way of explanation, the solar balloon, which uses a propane burner for initial heating and for whenever it is too cloudy, is made up of two envelopes. There is an external transparent envelope made out of a complex film of polyester resin in Dacron, with a volume of 5000

cubic meters, and an internal envelope made out of black Dacron that acts as a sun collector, with a volume of 4000 cubic meters. The air is heated using the global warming principle: the internal envelope transforms visible solar radiation into infrared radiation, which remains imprisoned inside the transparent envelope and is opaque to infrared radiation. This balloon was designed by Dominic Michaelis, a solar construction architect, at the beginning of 1981. On August 22nd, 1981 the aeronaut Julien Nott crossed the Channel on board a balloon of this type.

According to Don Cameron, however, "At the moment this balloon is not yet very practical."

The British aeronaut is always in search of new formulas to make balloons more accessible for everybody but, according to him, "Apart from three fields of application – sports, adver-

tising and passenger transport, I can't see any other areas of deployment, not even for scientific purposes."

As far as the future is concerned, could a balloon even be used on Jupiter?

In the United States a laboratory supported by NASA has developed a so-called "Aerobot" (AEROvehicle for planetary roBOTic exploration). Aerobots have some characteristics that differentiate them from traditional balloons: an autonomous position and the ability to determine the altitude and the climbing speed without any intervention from the ground. An Aerobot can actively control its own capabilities, it can follow a pre-determined flight path in the atmosphere using active altitude control and different wind conditions and, above all, it has the capability to land in pre-determined sites.

The Aerobot's applications depend on the

scientific objectives, such as observation under cloud formations that obstruct radio waves, surveying the relief of a planet, observation of hot atmospheres or wind conditions.

The inflation of the balloon envelope will differ depending on whether the planet is a terrestrial (solid) type of planet, like Mars, Earth, or Venus, or a Gas Giant (gaseous or fluid type of planet) like Jupiter, Saturn, Uranus, or Neptune. In the atmosphere of a terrestrial planet, it will be a gas balloon, that is to say that it will be inflated with a gas that is lighter than air, such as hydrogen or helium. For a gaseous planet, the balloon will be filled with ambient air, like a hot air balloon. The air will then be heated by an absorber of infrared rays on the envelope. All this remains fantasy for now, however, and part of the utopia of some "mad inventors" in the aeronautic field. And yet, nothing is impossible.

How does
it work

100-101 In Scotland, during the "Whisky Tour" on the Isle of Luing; before heating the interior of the envelope, the pilot proceeds to inflate the 3000-cubic meter balloon with cold air, using a fan.

lighter than air

THE MAGIC OF FLYING

How does it work? It is very simple: an envelope is inflated with hot air and because hot air has a lower volumetric mass in comparison to the air in the atmosphere, the balloon rises. The aerostatic flight is based on the Archimedes's principle: "a body immersed wholly or partially in fluid, experiences an upthrust force equal to the weight of the fluid displaced." This means that a balloon is immersed in the atmospheric fluid, and once inflated with gas, which is lighter than the air surrounding it, it receives a push upwards equal to the weight of the quantity of the atmospheric air corresponding to its volume.

If the push is higher than the weight of the balloon, the balloon ascends into the atmosphere. This means that in order to achieve a sufficient push for the balloon to ascend, it is necessary that the gas with which the balloon is inflated is lighter than the air of the atmosphere and that it surpasses the equilibrium point, namely the point at which the net weight of the balloon is equal to the weight of the air which is displaced. In this way, thanks to the action of the heat, the air in the hot air balloon expands. It is possible to verify this phenomenon in a still room by placing a thermometer on the floor and another one on the ceiling. This will show that there is a slight difference in the temperatures and that the air at the ceiling is warmer than the air on the ground.

A modern hot air balloon consists of three main elements: the envelope, the burner, connected to propane tanks, and the basket. The hot air ensures a upward force of about 275 grams/cu m, about a quarter of the force obtained by helium, so that a balloon of 77,962 cu ft (2,200 cu m) impresses an upward push of about 1,300 lb (600 kg), and a gas balloon of only 21,189 cu ft (600 cu m) will be sufficient to raise the same weight. For this reason, the modern hot air balloon can ascend or descend simply by increasing or decreasing the heat transmitted by the burner. The temperature of the hot air inside the hot air balloon varies between 176 and 212°F (80–100°C) and in order to fly this means that for the aerostatic push to be maintained by the burner, which warms up the air inside, the temperature should exceed by 140–176°F (60–80°C) the outer temperature. This means that if the air inside is not continually warmed then it will get cooler and the balloon will begin to descend. If the pilot does not warm it up, the balloon will accelerate the speed of descending, considering that the equilibrium point is reached at 16 ft (5 m)/second. Once this point is reached the balloon acts as a parachute.

In order to fully appreciate a hot air balloon flight, it is preferable to take off at first light. Then you will have the whole morning ahead of you to float on the thermals as they steadily develop with the strengthening sun. Furthermore, at sunrise the air is much fresher in comparison to the evening, and generally also the wind is calmer.

Moreover, as many pilots will tell you, everyone deserves an early morning flight in a hot air balloon. Why? The weather frequently obliges to provide the best conditions for enjoying a trip. Everything begins at sunrise. The pilot chooses a place, usually protected, for the take-off. Then, assisted by his assistant, who will follow in a 4x4 vehicle during the flight, called the recovery vehicle, and by the passengers, the pilot unloads the basket. Afterwards he installs the burner and tests that it is functioning properly with a large and noisy flame (this also serves to familiarize first-time ballooners to the burner, which can be startling).

Then the basket is put on the ground and, after having taken it out of its case, the envelope is hooked up to the spring clips of the load panel. Once spread out, the pilot starts the ventilator to insert air inside. The envelope blows up and assumes the familiar shape. The pilot turns on the burner and begins to warm up the air, while the other members of the crew hold the crown rope and the hot-air balloon straightens and rises. It is a surreal spectacle, extraordinary every single time due to the size of a balloon. Now the passengers can embark for an unforgettable adventure.

102 TOP LEFT A PILOT HEATS THE AIR OF HIS BALLOON DURING A RALLY OF THE CHÂTEAU D'OEX FESTIVAL IN SWITZERLAND.

102 TOP CENTER DURING INFLATION THE GONDOLA RESTS ON THE GROUND AT THE BIENNIAL WORLD BALLOON FESTIVAL IN ALSACE LORRAINE, FRANCE.

102 TOP RIGHT THE CREW MUST SUPPORT THE OPENING AT THE BASE OF THE ENVELOPE, THE SO-CALLED "MOUTH," TO AVOID BURNING THE MATERIAL DURING INFLATION.

102-103 ONCE THE ENVELOPE OF THE BALLOON IS INFLATED WITH COLD AIR, THE PILOT ACTIVATES THE BURNER TO HEAT THE AIR AND MAKE THE BALLOON RISE.

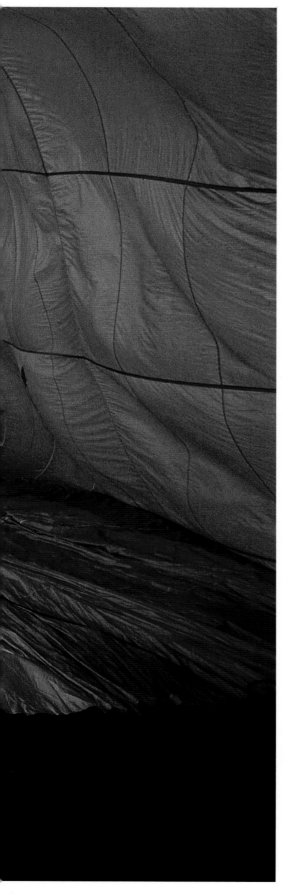

THE ENVELOPE

The envelope has the task of retaining the air that has been warmed-up by the burner. Its structure is constituted by horizontal and vertical panels (gores), which form a sphere. The envelopes are sewn together and are made of a synthetic fabric such as ripstop nylon, which is extremely strong. The fabric is coated with a film that makes it water-resistant and protects it against the effects of sunlight and the from the heat inside the envelope, which can reach a temperature of 230°F (110°C). All major panels of the envelope are reinforced with load tapes of nylon or polyester, developed to ensure very high standards reliability. The horizontal tapes limit the spread of any tears should they occur. All the vertical tapes are collected at the top on a ring or "crown ring," and they are secured at the base by means of steel ropes, which are fixed on the "load ring." The top of the envelope, which is open, is closed on the inner part by a mobile circular panel called "parachute" or "parachute valve." This valve, under the push of the hot air, gets flat on the top of the envelope and, fixed with Velcro fastener, seales it. It can also act as a valve that can be opened by pulling a red-white rope that runs on a pulley and attached to the fixing ropes of the parachute. The steering rope runs through a second pulley in order to amplify the tension to the maximum. In order to release the air and to steer the balloon, the parachute is slightly opened for a few seconds; for deflation it is pulled open and held in this position until the envelope is completely deflated.

The fabric panels at the base of the balloon are made of Nomex, a fabric characterized by high thermal resistance, and the nylon is kept at a sufficient distance from the flame in order to avoid being burnt. The lower ends of the load tapes form connection rings fixed on stainless-steel cables or ropes of Kevlar, which are called envelope tapes. The scoop (the triangle of tissue at the base of the envelope) can be adjusted to improve the performance of the balloon at the moment of taking off, help with the anchorage in conditions of strong winds, or during the flight in conditions of turbulence. Generally, the conventional shape of the envelope is described as "a reversed water drop."

The volume of hot air balloons varies between 35,000 and 350,000 cu ft (1,000 and 10,000 cu m), but some professional pilots have even bigger balloons. Nowadays, the most common hot air balloons have a volume of 77,962 cu ft (2,200 cu m). The flight duration depends obviously on the gas reserves, which can be loaded onto the basket. A pilot can choose where to take off, but he never knows where he will land, because for more than 200 years hot-air balloons have not been steered, but are at the mercy of the winds. On the other hand, an experienced pilot can control perfectly the altitude, almost to the inch, which, in conditions of calm wind, permits extraordinary flights over the countryside and exact soft landings. The average flight duration is about one or two hours and depends on the external temperature and on the fuel loaded.

106 TOP A MEMBER OF THE CREW ATTACHES THE VALVE AT THE TOP
OF THE ENVELOPE WITH VELCRO.

106 BOTTOM AND 106-107 DETAILS OF THE GORES THAT MAKE
UP THE ENVELOPE OF THE BALLOON.

108-109 AND 109 THE INSIDE OF A SPECIALLY SHAPED BALLOON IS COMPLEX, LIKE THIS BAGPIPE PLAYER, SEEN HERE DURING INFLATION AT CHÂTEAU D'OEX, IN SWITZERLAND. THE PILOT, MUIR MOFFAT (RIGHT) MUST USE ROPES TO FIX THE VELCRO PANELS THAT ARE USED TO DEFLATE THE BALLOON RAPIDLY.

110-111 DURING INFLATION OF THE BALLOON ENVELOPE, A MEMBER OF THE CREW MAKES SURE THAT THE PARACHUTE VALVE IS IN THE CORRECT POSITION.

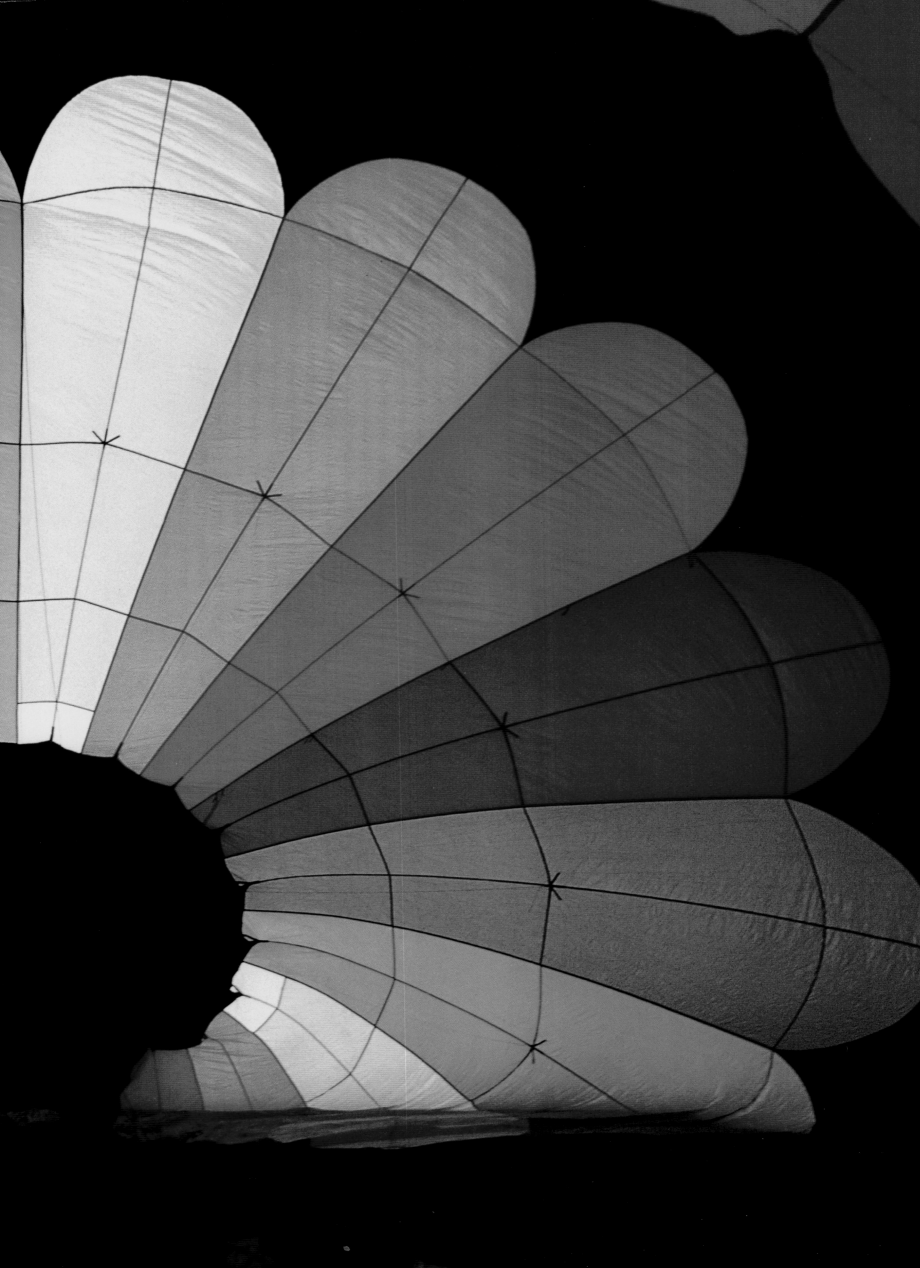

112-113 AT THE INTERNATIONAL "ZIPPO CUP" RALLY, MEMBERS OF
THE CREW CHECK THE VELCRO FASTENINGS OF THE BALLOON VALVE.

113 TOP DURING THE "ZIPPO CUP" MEETING A MEMBER OF THE
CREW HOLDS THE BALLOON BY THE CROWN LINE, WHILE THE BALLOON
RISES THANKS TO THE EFFECT OF THE HOT AIR.

113 BOTTOM DETAIL OF THE CROWN RING, WHICH IS POSITIONED
AT THE TOP OF THE BALLOON WHEN IT IS INFLATED.

THE BASKET

Traditionally, baskets are made of weaved wicker or bulrush. The bottom may also be weaved or made of wood veneers. The weight of the structure is supported by stainless steel ropes, which form a harness that begins at the the load ring and runs under the bottom of the basket. Baskets are reinforced by U-shaped tubes of aluminum or by a framework of steel, and they are fixed to the balloon by means of spring clips. The edges of the basket are stuffed with dense foam and are reinforced by leather or suede. The lower edges are covered with leather that protects the basket from damage, which can occur during landing or when being transported. There are several holes for the passage of the straps, which fix the cylinders (fuel tanks) and the platforms to enable people to get into the basket. The tapes of the basket, the supporting ribs, and the fuel pipes are within zipped, padded cases. Inside the basket there is padding on the bottom and sides for the comfort of the passengers. There is one fire extinguisher, fixed inside the basket.

Cameron Balloons in Bristol manufactures baskets divided in compartments which can accommodate between 10 and 20 passengers. These big baskets have internal compartments joined to the walls and the bottom. The compartments provide great structural integrity and separate the passengers. The pilot and the fuel cylinders occupy a compartment separated from the passengers. These big baskets divided into compartments use two points of fastening on every angle of the load ring in order to increase the resistance.

The biggest baskets with compartments also have eight supporting ribs, each with its own point of fastening, allowing for greater load capacity. It is possible to use a protective lining in order to cover the flexible tubes which run from the center of the load ring to the center of the pilot's compartment. Hot air balloons that have a basket divided into compartments should have some rotation panels in order to orientate the basket so that its length can be set perpendicular to the axis of the wind at the moment of the landing.

116-117 The gondolas have different dimensions according to the size of the balloon. In the photograph is a gondola that can carry 15 people, at the World Biennial in Alsace Lorraine, in France.

117 Detail of the load ring of a gas balloon during the Sint-Niklaas Rally.

118 top A MEMBER OF THE CREW OPENS THE "MOUTH"
OF THE ENVELOPE WHILE THE PILOT LIGHTS THE BURNER
TO HEAT THE COLD AIR INSIDE THE BALLOON.

118 top center MEMBERS OF THE CREW ARE READY TO HOLD
DOWN THE BALLOON WHILE IT IS INFLATED WITH HOT AIR.

118 top right A PILOT ACTIVATES THE BURNER.

118-119 IN GENERAL, BALLOONS HAVE A DOUBLE BURNER
FOR SAFETY REASONS, FUELED BY PROPANE GAS.

THE BURNER
AND THE CYLINDERS

The heating source in a hot air balloon is a very powerful burner that uses liquid propane. The burner releases a 10–20-ft (3–6-m) flame, directed with precision into the envelope through the bottom opening called the mouth. The burner, mounted on a load ring, can be moved so that the pilot can always correctly position the flame right in the middle of the mouth of the envelope.

A flexible tube connects the burner to the cylinders (fuel tanks). Modern-day hot air balloons usually have two burners. The cylinders, which once were made in aluminium, now are made in steel, or titanium and contain between 44 and 110 lb (20 and 50 kg) of liquid propane. Many manufacturers carry out continuous reserch for new materials, looking for cylinders more and more light. The opening of the cyclinders' valves releases the propane (-43.5°F) which, prior to combustion, passes through a vaporization system and, due to the heat, distributes it to the burner's nozzles, where it is spread in order to mix up with the air and burn by contact with the main flame. The fuel flow is managed by a valve called the heating or main valve. Generally, this heating valve is distinguished by a red color (in the model made by Cameron).

The propane, petrol, or kerosene burner warms up the air contained in the balloon. Single, double, triple, and even quadruple burners are used according to the volume of the envelope. Each nozzle has a gauge that indicates the pressure of the fuel being delivered to the burner. The right pressure varies between 4.5 and 7 bars. In order to obtain the optimum performance of the burner, the pressure for propane should never fall under 3.5 bars. However, propane pressure drops in the cold, so in winter it is necessary to protect the cylinders against the cold, or to add nitrogen to the mix to maintain the pressure at 7 bars.

A burner may have a secondary valve known as a "whisper burner," which feeds the combustible liquid directly to a nozzle with multiple holes and produces a quieter flame. The fuel flow is regulated by a revolving valve or by a pivoting valve, which can change the performance of the burner. Normally this silent burner is used when the balloon flies over livestock so that it does not scare them with the noise of a normal burner. This type of burner was developed for occasional use, otherwise it will produce deposit of soot on the inside of the envelope.

The fuel tanks that contain the liquid propane under pressure are the cylinders. These can come in two configurations: "standard," working exclusively with liquid fuel, and "master," which has an additional supply of gas for the pilot flame.

The propane is picked from a tube, which plunges on the bottom of the cylinder. The output of the supply is controlled both by a tap having a fitting of the type Rego, and by means of a "quarter turn" tap, which is sphere-shaped and is activated by a lever. The lastly mentioned tap is realized with fittings Rego or quick fittings Thema.

The adjustable gas supply of the pilot flame, only through the master cylinder, is performed directly from the cylinder cap by means of a tap and an adjustable pressure reducer. The tube of the gas is connected to a quick fitting.

The cylinder are fixed vertically by means of belts inside the basket, generally in the four angles. If there are used cylinders of 60 or 80 litres, on the wicker floor should be installed a bottom for the distribution of charge.

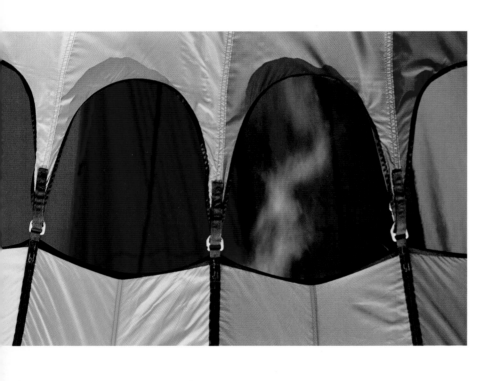

120 DETAIL OF A PART OF A BALLOON ENVELOPE. THE BURNER FLAME IS IN THE BACKGROUND.

120-121 A PILOT ACTIVATES THE BURNER DURING THE CARPINETI RALLY, IN THE PROVINCE OF REGGIO EMILIA, IN ITALY.

The major meetings

balloon rally

THE GREAT ESCAPE

In 1972 the city of Albuquerque, New Mexico hosted the first balloon rally. It marked the rebirth of an aerostatic sport that had been abandoned many years earlier following various incidents. In the United States some engineers re-invented the balloon by introducing many new principles and techniques, but maintaining the same identical principle: using hot air to fly by balloon.

Over the years, with the return of balloons in Europe, particularly in France where they were invented by the Montgolfier brothers, rallies (now called meetings) were organized one after another.

Most of the big meetings have now been around for quite some time, like the Bristol Rally or the event at Château-d'Oex in Switzerland that celebrated its 30th anniversary in 2008.

For many pilots at the beginning of their careers, the "young burners" as they are known in ballooning slang, participating in a meeting is reassuring. For minor competitive events, a pilot attends a briefing during which the flight plans, meteorological conditions and the objectives of the trial are explained, which allows a young pilot to perfect his or her knowledge without any problems. A meeting also means meeting other pilots, who often only see each other on such occasions. This allows the exchange of ideas about flying and new technology.

Rallies have multiplied all over the world over the last 20 years, even in Eastern Europe. Since the fall of the Berlin Wall, frontiers are open and these new countries, which remained hidden away in the dark for many years, offer pilots new places to explore. For some time now rallies have been held in Lithuania, Slovakia, Croatia, Hungary and Poland. Pilots from former communist countries are also eager to participate in meetings in Europe and in France. Hardly a weekend goes by in these countries without a balloon meeting. Moreover, at the time of the "mad cow" disease in Britain, pilots were no longer authorized to fly in that country, so they were happy to cross the English Channel to go and fly over the French countryside. At the world rally in Chambley, held in the month of August, there had never been so many English pilots as there were during those years.

We must not forget that the success of a meeting today depends on just the right chemistry when pilots and spectators meet. Therefore, rallies all over the world have a theme or a special feature to attract pilots and their crews. The mountains of Château-d'Oex, the castles in the Loire Valley at the François Ier Trophée, the record number of balloons in Albuquerque, or the traditional charm of Sint-Niklaas, the oldest rally in Europe, all have their special charm.

château-d'oex

A STORY OF PASSION

In order for a ballooning event to last for 30 years it has to have the passion and commitment of people who believe in its success. At Château-d'Oex, Switzerland, as well as elsewhere, such as Sint-Niklaas in Belgium or Albuquerque, New Mexico, if there had not been a man with a strong will and indomitable spirit driving the project forward it would never have been realized. Château-d'Oex was losing popularity due to the fewer numbers of tourists visiting the area until someone developed the idea of making the municipality more dynamic and attractive through its tourist office. Charles André Ramseier and some friends discovered the Albuquerque International Balloon Fiesta, the biggest meeting of its kind in the world, which is held in the desert of New Mexico. Each year hundreds of balloons take off every morning over the 10 days of the event. Ramseier appreciated the wonderful carnival atmosphere, where the balloon pilots, rather like rodeo cowboys, took off every morning with a contagious feeling of euphoria. It is still night, the sky is dark, illuminated only by the "Dawn Patrols," the balloons that fly at sunrise, and already there is a multicolored fiesta pulsating to the rhythm of "country music." Ramseier thought: "If we succeed in introducing such an event into the mountains, the addition of our panorama would make the effect extraordinary!" He returned from the United States with his mind full of ideas.

Only 30 years ago in France and Switzerland the number of hot air balloon pilots could be counted on the fingers of one hand. It was necessary to start from scratch with everything. However, sometimes destiny makes the right things happen at the right time. A meeting with a German pilot would launch hot air ballooning activity in the district of Pays d'Enhaut, of which Château-d'Oex is the capital. Ramseier dragged the pilot to a café on the corner where important negotiations and contracts are usually concluded. The discussion between the director of the Tourist Office of Château-d'Oex and the German Hans Büker lasted one-and-a-half hours. Büker had experienced the pleasure of ballooning in 1969 and from that moment the passion for it had never left him. Actually, this is the way many people become avid pilots. They gain some experience and they are captured by the thrill of it and the passion takes them over.

On Sunday, October 8, 1978, for the first time a hot air balloon took off from Château-d'Oex. The director of the Tourist Office proposed to the German pilot that he remain in Château-d'Oex to develop an event to promote the flights to the tourists. From the very beginning there was an excellent relationship between them and Ramseier saw the possibility of using hot air balloon flights to stimulate tourism during winter. Not completely satisfied by the passenger flights in the valley, the director of the Tourist Office aimed to achieve much more, because the small winter sports station could not count on a serious tourist flow during the winter.

"What about organizing an international hot air balloon week?" It was already November and the proposed event could be inaugurated in February. The final decision to organize the fiesta was taken at the beginning of December, which left about two months to plan the event. Hans Büker was responsible for the "technical" planning, while the Tourist Office managed the administration, the authorizations, the funding, and the advertising. In Switzerland, as it would be anywhere else, it was necessary to convince the relevant authorities, because of the novelty of hot air ballooning at that time and basically nobody knew what was involved in organizing a balloon fiesta.

On February 10, 1979, 14 pilots arrived in Château-d'Oex for the first "International hot air balloon week." The balloon spectacle started on the weekend and during the week the pilots took part in air competitions. Thirty-one years later the formula has not changed, to the great pleasure of the spectators and pilots. Charles André Ramseier did not believe that 31 years later balloons would still be appearing in the skies of Pays d'Enhaut.

However, today over 100 balloons appear in the third week of January and the spectacle is magnificent, with air acrobatics, hang-gliders, which detach from the balloons, and pilots who unhook parachutists. The spectators, some 30,000, marvel at the delightful ballet of multicolored bubbles.

An added attraction is the night show, which involves using the burner flames to create a choreographed display of flames and light, which is supervised every year by Laurent Exchaquet. It was launched about 10 years ago under the name of "Candles in the Valley" and today it has becomes a sophisticated and dazzling event of hot air balloon theater in the depths of nature. While the night comes down over Château-d'Oex, the pilots inflate the envelopes on the south side of the Pays d'Enhaut

128-129 *Inflating balloons in the small launch field at Château-d'Oex is always a very impressive spectacle.*

129 *Bertrand Piccard, who completed his first round-the-world balloon trip, on the occasion of the inauguration of the Château-d'Oex Festival, in Switzerland.*

130-131 *The Rally at Château-d'Oex, a small ski resort in the Vaud Alps at an altitude of 1000 meters, is an annual event.*

mountains. A stream of traffic meanders through the streets to reach the winter station, and the hill of the Temple is crowded with excited spectators who come to marvel at the spectacle of the hot air balloons illuminated in the night.

The master of ceremonies is Laurent Exchaquet, who directs this large-scale piece of theater with its awesome backdrop of mountains covered by a thick white blanket. The firing of a cannon resonates around the mountains and the burners of the hot air balloons are fired up. The spectacle begins and the light from the roaring burners illuminates the whole village. And then, as if touched by a magic wand, everything turns off and from the mountains come down falling stars. These are the paragliders of the Château-d'Oex sports club, which illuminate the night sky with their sparkling arabesques. The spectacle is complete, the public are enchanted and do not know where to look, because the hot air balloons are flaming in all directions.

During this magical and incredible display, which combines pyrotechnical effects and air acrobatics, spectators spot the lighting of four giant hot air balloons floating at 650 ft (200 m), outlined by the light from their burners, which reflects onto the mountains below. Back on the ground, on the sports fields, a group of acrobats dance on stilts 9–12 ft (3–4 m) high in front of an illuminated balloon. While the hot air balloons flicker to the rhythm of the music, the "elf-skiers," ski down the slopes carrying torches, executing figures between the balloons.

The spectacle reaches its peak and as the burners are turned off the crowds roar their appreciation. The exact number of spectators to these night events is unknown, but many come from distant locations to watch this balloon extravaganza high in the mountains which has brought fame to Château-d'Oex.

Thousands of visitors invade the streets and the square of the village to continue the party, all the shops remain open, and various spectacles continue until late into the night.

132-133 THE SMALL RESORT OF CHÂTEAU-D'OEX ENJOYS AN EXTRAORDINARY MICRO-CLIMATE AND BALLOONS CAN TAKE OFF THERE AGAINST A CLOUDLESS BLUE SKY.

133 TOP A SWISS COW FLIES BETWEEN THE MOUNTAINS OF CHÂTEAU-D'OEX.

133 CENTER THE FESTIVAL OF CHÂTEAU-D'OEX OFFERS SPECTATORS A MAGNIFICENT AERIAL BALLET.

133 BOTTOM A BALLOON TAKES OFF ON THE STARTER'S ORDERS. THE STARTER GUARANTEES SAFETY ON THE GROUND.

134 WHEN FOLDING A BALLOON AT CHÂTEAU-D'OEX, IT IS ALWAYS ADVISABLE TO LAND ON A ROAD.

134-135 LANDING WITH THE GONDOLA AND THE ENVELOPE ON THE SNOW-COVERED ROADS FACILITATES ACCESS FOR CARS THAT HAVE TO COLLECT THE MATERIAL.

136-137 A CAR IS READY TO LEAVE FOR THE SKY DURING THE RALLY AT CHÂTEAU-D'OEX.

138-139 THIS BLACK FIGURE SEEMS TO BE SAYING "CUCKOO! HERE I AM!" AN EFFECT OF THE STITCHING AND THE LITTLE WINK OF THE EYE ON THE ENVELOPE OF THE BALLOON.

139 THE MICHELIN "BIBENDUM" BALLOONS HAVE MADE A SLIGHT DETOUR TO CHÂTEAU-D'OEX.

140-141 AT THE CHÂTEAU-D'OEX MEETING DURING TAKEOFF, BALLOONS CAN COME INTO CONTACT WITH EACH OTHER, BUT IT IS NOT DANGEROUS.

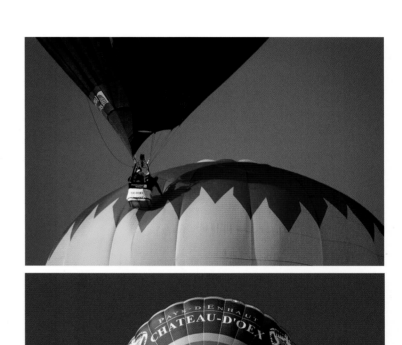

142-143 *Takeoff at Château-d'Oex: the gondola with the banner of the rally advertises the resort.*

143 top *At Château-d'Oex there are always accidents: the gondola of one balloon brushes against the top of another balloon.*

143 bottom *One of the balloons with the colors of Château-d'Oex, the rally organizing resort, has just taken off into the blue sky.*

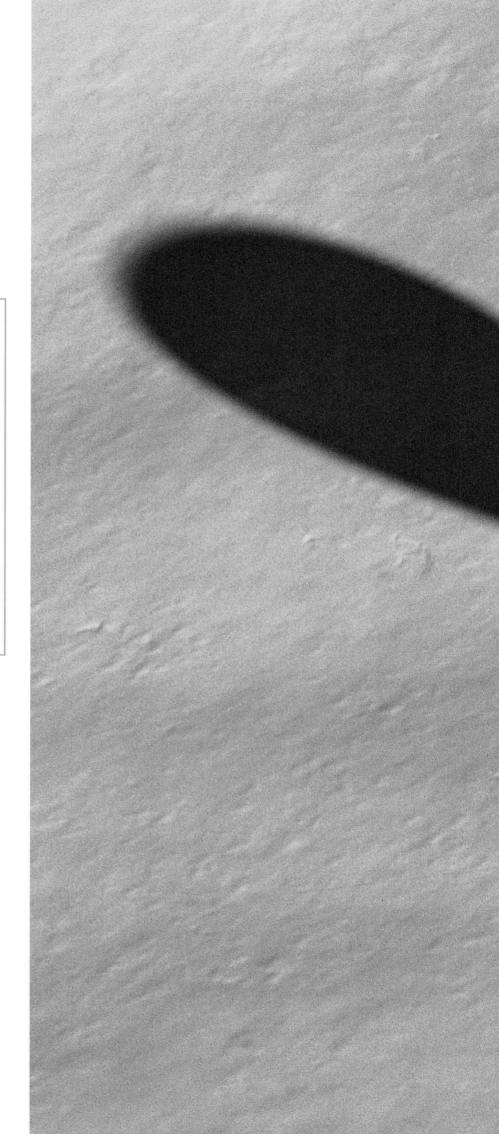

144 *A balloon seen from above, as it flies over the main street in Château-d'Oex.*

144-145 *The shadow of the balloon skims over a farm in the Pays d'Enhaut in Château-d'Oex.*

146-147 A BALLOON OF THE BOMBARD COMPANY, WHICH TAKES CARE OF TRANSPORTING PASSENGERS TO CHÂTEAU D'OEX, FLIES BETWEEN THE MOUNTAINS.

147 TOP THE BALLOON OF BELGIUM'S ROY SAX FLIES OVER THE FIR TREES COVERED IN THE SNOW OF THE SWISS ALPS.

147 BOTTOM THE "HONDA-AZIMO" BALLOON IN THE SKY OVER CHÂTEAU-D'OEX TAKES OFF AMID A STUNNING PANORAMA.

the françois Ier trophy

A ROYAL FLIGHT

The newest of the prestigious meetings is the François Ier Trophy, which takes place usually during the last week of May in the skies over the châteaux of the Loire, France. It was established in 1991 by a few pilots who wished to see the châteaux from hot air balloons. Today, this 10-day event attracts pilots from all over the world who enjoy appreciating the wonderful heritage of this region of France in such a novel way.

Established by Jean Becker, president of "Ballooning Adventures", this friendly race could always rely on the attendance of journalists to witness the show. More than 500 journalists are invited to be passengers in the balloons and to take with them their cameras to share with their readers the splendor of the landscape below as they float over the Loire and Sologne rivers. The meeting has always been reserved mainly for foreign pilots who want to discover the region, and so many Americans, Canadians, Africans, and Asians gather in one of the most beautiful regions of France, which was a favorite with royalty and nobility. During the week the pilots fly over the magnificent château of Chambord, which is the residence of François I, for whom the show is named. Nowadays, the François Ier Trophy attracts pilots who are famous for the competitions they have won and for their great experience. Every year there are participants from a dozen different countries. It is an occasion for the pilots to test themselves in a friendly way, playing with the winds in the sky above the Sologne. They are aware that these tests determine the best pilots on the basis of the precision of their skills at navigation. The purpose of the meeting is also to share the passion for aerostatic flights with the passengers and journalists, who are invited to fly during the show.

All of the take-offs from the various châteaux of the Sologne are spectacular, but those from Cheverny and Chenonceau are particularly unforgettable experiences. Moreover, since 2008, the hot air balloons take off from the superb park of Valençay, where Talleyrand lived. All the flights reveal the superb richness of the region, furthermore they offer a unique view of the life of the French kings who enjoyed staying here from François I to Louis XIV, as well as Napoleon III. Not to mention the wonderful gastronomy, thanks to the many famous chefs who welcome us at their tables, where it is not unusual to sit next to a marquis or a count. The proprietors of the Sologne châteaux have enthusiastically participated in this ballooning event since the beginning. Without them the meeting would lose most of its charm, both for the pilots and for the journalists, who delight in bringing together the wonderful spectacle of balloons and châteaux; a thrilling combination.

150-151 THE BALLOONS LEAVE
FROM THE CASTLE OF BEAUREGARD,
NOT FAR FROM BLOIS.

151 TOP FOUR BALLOONS MEET
FOR THE TWINNING FLIGHT OF
FOUR RALLIES: SINT- NIKLAAS,
BRISTOL, CHÂTEAU-D'OEX,
AND ROMORANTIN.

One evening in 2001, during a Scotch whisky tasting in the small castle of Muir Moffat, Claude Jelk, a member of the committee organizing the Château-d'Oex meeting, got the idea to twin his event with the one at Bristol. "Being two partners could help us to develop a synergy to organize our meetings better", explained Claude. The next day Muir mentioned his idea to Jean Sax, director of the Sint-Niklaas meeting. The proposal took time to develop. Finally, the three committee members agreed on the requirements for a common show. At the Château-d'Oex meeting in 2002 the twinning was sealed by the ascent of three balloons which were connected by means of banners. "It's a good idea", said Claude. "We could see each other more often to exchange ideas about aerostatic flights. Moreover, it will allow us to obtain greater fame." Claude had an obsession: to raise the profile of his small municipality in the hot air balloon world, especially among the international meetings. Two years later, Claude asked the committee of the François Ier Trophy to associate with the twinning. So in January 2003 a delegation from Loir-et-Cher, with Romorantin's balloon, and memebers of the "court" of François went to Château-d'Oex to participate in the twinning ceremony. Today, four meetings have associated: Sint-Niklaas (the most historic meeting in Europe), Bristol (the largest meeting in England), the François Ier Trophy (a prestigious show over the Loire châteaux), and Château-d'Oex (the meeting in the mountains). They are all different from each other and they maintain that distinctiveness.

This twinning process showed to the various municipal administrators just how important is their support to ensure the successful implementation of the balloon meetings and also for their long-term viability. One thing is certain, if there is a decline in ballooning then only the most prestigious meetings will survive. Muir would like to go further and create a European Grand Prix with national teams, which would participate in four meetings. The teams would take part in two selective races to win the Grand Prix. In this way a great international competition would be established without disturbing the popularity of the other meetings.

At the time of writing Muir and his friends have still to overcome the major obstacle of funding an extended competition, but they are confident that media attention of such a visual event would be sufficient to provide the financing. For example, the rights to cover the competition could be sold to a TV channel who would televise the races.

Today, the cities and their mayors support the twinning enthusiastically and municipal delegations meet regularly, both in England and France. Hot air balloons closely associated with the various cities where the meetings are held participate regularly in the four shows. However, all four of the mayors have still not succeeded in meeting all together in one place; this is the next challenge!

152 top The crews are ready for takeoff from the Castle of Chambord, from the ceremonial courtyard on the south side.

152 center Muir Moffat inflates the balloon in the shape of a bagpipe player in the park of the Castle of Beauvais in Romorantin.

152 bottom The François Ier Trophée offers the opportunity for a pleasant twinning of balloons and vintage cars like the Bugatti.

152-153 The Castle of Chambord was built for hunting by Francis I, after whom the François Ier Trophée was named, for the rally held at the castle in May every year. The takeoff from Chambord remains one of the main attractions of this unique event, which involves flying over the castles of the Loire, in the heart of Sologne.

154 AND 154-155 BALLOONS TAKE OFF EARLY IN THE MORNING FROM THE FIELDS AROUND THE CASTLE OF VALENÇAY FOR THE FRANÇOIS IER TROPHÉE DISPLAY ON JUNE 1ST, 2008.

156 TOP AND 156-157 FOR THE FRANÇOIS IER TROPHÉE, BALLOONS TAKE OFF AT SUNRISE FROM THE FIELDS OF VARIOUS CASTLES, INCLUDING CHEVERNY.

156 CENTER TAKEOFF FROM THE FIELD OF A CASTLE OFTEN REQUIRES GREAT SKILL ON THE PART OF THE PILOT, WHO MUST INFLATE THE ENVELOPE ON THE AVENUES OF PARKS AMIDST LARGE TREES.

156 BOTTOM EVEN THOUGH THEY TAKE OFF IN A GROUP, TRANSPORTED BY THE WINDS, THE PILOTS PROCEED TO DISCOVER THE UNSPOILT AND PROTECTED NATURE AROUND SOLOGNE IN TOTAL SOLITUDE.

158 top Taking off from Salbris, you can see the Castle of Rivaulde in the middle of the woods.

158 bottom The Romorantin Balloon is ready to take off from the Château du Moulin, in the heart of Sologne.

158-159 On a beautiful May morning the balloons take off from the Castle of Villemorant (Neung-sur-Beuvron, Sologne).

160-161 THE AEROSTATS TAKE OFF FROM THE FIELDS OF THE CASTLE THAT BELONGS TO THE DOUANES, IN LA FERTÉ-IMBAULT (SOLOGNE).

161 FLYING FOR THE FRANÇOIS IER TROPHÉE, CARRIED BY THE WIND, IN SOLOGNE YOU DISCOVER MANY SMALL PRIVATE CASTLES.

162   THE BALLOONS TAKE OFF FROM THE CENTER OF LA FERTÉ-BEAUHARNAIS, A SMALL, QUAINT VILLAGE IN SOLOGNE.

163   A PILOT PREPARES TO THROW THE MARKER ON A TARGET FOR THE FRIENDLY COMPETITION HELD ON THE OCCASION OF THE FRANÇOIS IER TROPHÉE.

164-165 FOR A WEEK THE BALLOONS PARTICIPATING IN THE FRANÇOIS IER TROPHÉE FLY OVER THE TYPICAL LANDSCAPE OF THE SOLOGNE, WITH MANY SMALL CASTLES SCATTERED IN THE WOODS.

165 TOP THE LANDSCAPE OF THE SOLOGNE REVEALS A REGION OF FORESTS AND SMALL LAKES.

165 BOTTOM A FINE BUILDING CONCEALED BEHIND THE WOODS, TYPICAL OF THE REGION, WHICH CAN ONLY BE SEEN FROM THE GONDOLAS OF BALLOONS.

bristol

THE CRADLE OF MODERN HOT AIR BALLOONING

In August 2008, the Bristol International Balloon Fiesta celebrated its 30th anniversary. In the course of the previous three years, the meeting had attracted not less than 500,000 spectators and somewhere between 100 and 120 hot air balloons, mainly from the UK with about 10 from abroad, which makes this essentially an English event. Bristol is very much the cradle of modern aerostatic flights, because it is there that Don Cameron established his balloon manufacturing business, and he also contributed enormously to establishing this event.

This great balloon festival lasts four days and there are also many other attractions, including a fairground, and during the day there are different events right up to the evening take-off. For the 30th anniversary, for example, the Red Arrows display team wowed the crowd with their stunning flying skills executed with surgical precision above their heads. What is remarkable is that sights such as the Red Arrows and the incredible hot-air balloon take-offs are all free. With the arrival of night, people of all ages arrive from all directions, near and far, to enjoy a breath-taking spectacle. About 30 balloons, tethered to the ground, become giant light bulbs as their burners are turned on and illuminate the night sky. The flames are fired and flared in keeping with the rhythm of accompanying music to the cheering delight of the spectators. This impressive event lasts for 30 minutes before reaching its climax with a firework display.

In the mornings and evenings, the public come to watch the mass ascents and on Thursday evening there is a special ascent reserved for the special-shaped balloons. The highlight of this take-off is always the "bagpipe player," which is the tallest special-shaped balloon and is piloted by Muir Moffat, who is one of the committee members of this great festival. A further specialty of this meeting is the presence of enormous balloons designed for passenger flights, which have baskets capable of carrying between 10 and 15 people. These balloons are of impressive dimensions and flown by experienced professional pilots.

168 top Many specially shaped balloons participate in Bristol. The main manufacturer of this type of aerostat is Don Cameron, who has a factory in the city.

168 center The "Bristol International Fiesta" starts on Thursday evening with the takeoff of the special shapes.

168 bottom In Bristol, which hosts almost 120 balloons, the moment of inflation makes you think of the "housing crisis".

168-169 The 120 balloons take off one after another from the "Ashton Court Park," west of Bristol. The French cock is being inflated on the ground.

170 *top* *Many cities host balloon rallies and the balloons carry the city colors with pride, as in this picture, taken in the sky over Bristol.*

170 *bottom* *A little house floats in the sky over the urban community of Bristol.*

170-171 *Bristol is located in the south-west of England, on the River Avon, which traditionally marked the boundaries between the counties of Gloucestershire and Somerset. Bristol has a population of 500,000 and is the sixth largest city in the country, but above all it is the English ballooning capital.*

172-173 A PANORAMA OF "ASHTON COURT PARK," WHERE
BALLOONS TAKE OFF AFTER MIDDAY ON SATURDAY ON THE OCCASION
OF THE BRISTOL FESTIVAL.

173 TOP NEW SPECIALLY SHAPED BALLOONS PARTICIPATE IN THE
"BRISTOL INTERNATIONAL FESTIVAL" EVERY YEAR.

173 BOTTOM A SMILING STEAM LOCOMOTIVE RISES IN THE
BRISTOL SKY.

174-175 INFLATING A SPECIALLY SHAPED BALLOON IS NOT EASY AND, AS IN THE CASE OF THE SCOTTISH BAGPIPE PLAYER IN THE PHOTO, IT CAN TAKE SEVERAL HOURS.

175 TOP THE PILOT HOLDS THE MOUTH OF THE ENVELOPE OPEN IN ORDER TO FACILITATE THE ENTRANCE OF AIR COMING FROM THE FAN.

175 BOTTOM THE MEMBERS OF THE CREW, OF WHICH SEVERAL ARE REQUIRED TO INFLATE A SPECIALLY SHAPED BALLOON, STRUGGLE TO ATTACH THE VELCRO RIBBONS THAT HOLD THE PARACHUTE VALVE IN PLACE.

176 TOP AN ACROBAT ON A MOTORBIKE SUSPENDED FROM A GONDOLA DOES HIS ACT IN THE BRISTOL SKY.

176 CENTER "CHURCHILL," THE MASCOT OF THE INSURANCE COMPANY OF THE SAME NAME, FLIES OVER THE CITY OF BRISTOL.

176 BOTTOM AFTER FLYING OVER THE CITY OF BRISTOL, BEFORE LANDING, THE BALLOONS SET OUT TO DISCOVER THE ENGLISH COUNTRYSIDE.

176-177 AFTER FLYING FOR A QUARTER OF AN HOUR IN THE AUGUST SKY, THE BALLOONS REACH THE CLIFTON SUSPENSION BRIDGE IN BRISTOL.

the biennial of the aerostatic flights

HEAVENLY LORRAINE

Jean-François Pilâtre de Rozier was a major figure in the history of aerostatic flight, as important as the Montgolfier brothers. In 1983, on the 200th anniversary of his first flight, the Pilâtre de Rozier Challenge was first held in Metz. In 1989, during the bicentenary celebrations of the French Revolution, the committee members decided to organize in Lorraine a balloon meeting in the same league as the one held in Albuquerque. Initially, it was to be just a single meeting, not to be repeated, and it was certainly not intended to become a biennial event.

The show was planned in two stages. The first to be held in Lorraine and the second in the *département* of Hauts de Seine. However, for various reasons, the show was only held in Lorraine. For almost two months, the committee members searched for a suitable place for the meeting, and finally they chose the site of the future Lorraine airport, located between Pagny-les-Goin and Goin (between Metz and Nancy). Work on the airport had bot begun and feelings among the local communities ran strong and there were many anti-airport demonstrations. But it was decided that it was here that the new balloon show "Fraternité 89" should be held. Although it was only ever intended as a single event, such was its success that two years later a another show was established on the runways of the future regional airport of Metz-Nancy. Although it was obvious that holding the event every year would not be practical, the alternative of a biennial meeting proved to be acceptable. From 1989 to 1991 there were two shows on the site of the airport. In 1993 it was held in the heart of Lorraine's nature park, and then the show was moved to a former American airbase, Chambley, which had been used between 1953 and 1967.

The shows of 1993, 1995, and 1997 were all a great success, even though their ephemeral nature meant that there was no infrastructure for long-term continuity. In 1999, an added attraction in the middle of the day was the solar eclipse. This extraordinary moment was marveled at by the thousands of spectators. The event also lived up to its stated intention of matching Albuquerque's mass ascencions with hundreds of hot air balloons ready to take flight (making a world record in 2005). Then came the night inflations, a really impressive event, and even more spectacular were the night ascents, which created a magical atmosphere of adventure and wonder.

The 2007 edition of the Lorraine Mondial Air Ballons, as the rally has been termed, was a success from all points of view. The Lorraine rally hosted 1187 pilots and 961 balloons with crews from 38 different nations.

Today, as its founder, Philippe Buron Pilâtre, is fond of saying, the Lorraine Mondial Air Ballons is "the most international balloon rally in the world." The rally, which took place from Friday July 27th to August 5th, 2007, welcomed almost 350,000 visitors to the Chambley Air Base. Over the 10 days of the rally, 14 of the 19 programmed flights were made. Two thousand and seven will always be a special year in the memory of those pilots who participated.

180-181 DURING THE 10 DAYS OF THE BALLOON BIENNIAL FESTIVAL, HUNDREDS OF BALLOONS TAKE OFF IN THE MIST EVERY MORNING.

181 TOP AT THE BIENNIAL BALLOONING FESTIVAL, THE BALLOONS TAKE OFF FROM THE FORMER NATO MILITARY BASE IN CHAMBLEY, NEAR METZ.

181 BOTTOM THE BALLOONS FLY ABOVE THE COUNTRYSIDE OF ALSACE-LORRAINE, AS PART OF THE FESTIVAL THAT BEGAN IN 1989.

182-183 In the morning, at the Biennial Balloon Festival, during takeoff from the field of Chambley there is total confusion and the field is a mass of balloon envelopes.

183 top The crews prepare for takeoff: during inflation the balloon begins to rise.

183 center The balloons, usually on the same line of departure, rise as they inflate one after another.

183 bottom Third phase of inflation: the balloons are ready and waiting for the starting signal to take off.

184-185 THE SHOW IS GUARANTEED, NOT ONLY FOR THE BALLOONS BUT ALSO FOR THE TRAILERS DECORATED WITH THE SAME COLORS AS THE AEROSTATS, IN THIS CASE WITH A "WESTERN" LANDSCAPE.

185 A TRAILER WITH THE COLORS OF BELGIUM, WHICH, WITH THE BALLOON OF THE VEHICLE'S OWNER, CONTRIBUTES TO CREATING THE TYPICAL ATMOSPHERE OF THE BALLOONING BIENNIAL.

186-187 Like all big gatherings held all over the world, the World Ballooning Biennial also features special shapes.

187 top The red horse, the symbol of the Swedish county of Dalarna, is ready to take off at the Ballooning Biennial.

187 center The special shapes are inflated at the same time as the other balloons.

187 bottom In 2007, for the 20th anniversary of the festival in Alsace Lorraine, the organizers invited a balloon in the shape of a birthday cake.

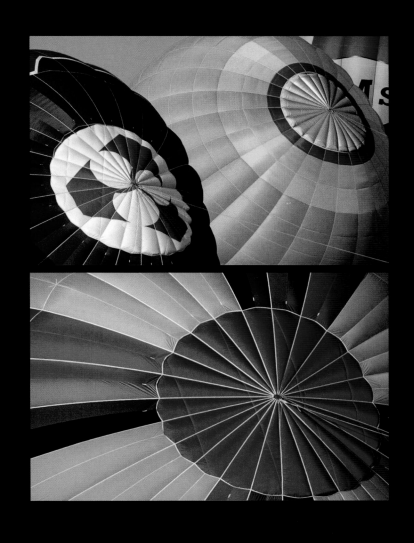

188-189 THE BALLOONS ARE FILLED BY A FAN THAT SENDS COLD AIR INTO THE ENVELOPE.

189 TOP SOME BALLOON VALVES ARE DECORATED WITH THE SPONSOR'S COLORS; THESE BALLOONS CAN
BE RECOGNIZED WHILE THEY ARE BEING INFLATED ON THE GROUND.

189 BOTTOM INTERPLAY OF COLORS WITH THE VALVE, WHICH REMAINS FIRMLY ATTACHED TO THE
ENVELOPE OF THE BALLOON.

190-191 SPONSORS OR OWNERS OF BALLOONS DECORATE THEIR BALLOONS IN THE MOST ORIGINAL WAYS. ALL THE DECORATIONS ARE STITCHED, NOT PAINTED ON THE MATERIAL OF THE ENVELOPE.

191 EVEN THOUGH IT IS NOT A SPECIAL SHAPE, THIS BALLOON LOOKS LIKE A HOUSE.

192-193 THE GONDOLA OF A COMMERCIAL BALLOON, WITH EIGHT PASSENGERS, TAKES OFF IN FRONT OF THE MICHELIN BALLOON AND THE "BIBENDUM" WAVES TO THE PASSENGERS.

194 TOP *THE BALLOONS FLY IN THE ALSACE LORRAINE SKY ON THE OCCASION OF THE WORLD BALLOONING BIENNIAL IN 2007.*

194 BOTTOM *A RED AND BLACK LADYBIRD TAKES OFF IN THE EARLY MORNING MIST.*

194-195 *THE BALLOONS TAKE ADVANTAGE OF A BREEZE THAT CARRIES THEM IN THE DIRECTION OF THE LAKE OF MADINE, ABOUT TEN KILOMETERS FROM THE LAUNCH FIELD AT THE CHAMBLEY BASE.*

196-197 AT TAKEOFF, A BALLOON SEEN FROM THE GROUND SHOWS ITS DECORATIONS FROM A DIFFERENT PERSPECTIVE; IT IS POSSIBLE TO IDENTIFY THE CURVED LINES AND THE INCREASINGLY LARGE CIRCLES CAN BE CLEARLY DISTINGUISHED.

197 THE BALLOONS THAT PARTICIPATE IN THE RALLIES ARE USUALLY OF A SMALL SIZE AND, DEPENDING ON THEIR VOLUME, CAN TRANSPORT FROM TWO TO FOUR PASSENGERS.

198 top A BALLOON PREPARES TO LAND IN THE ALSACE LORRAINE COUNTRYSIDE.

198 bottom IN ALSACE LORRAINE IN SUMMER, THE HARVESTING SEASON IS OVER AND THE PILOTS CAN LAND THEIR BALLOONS WITHOUT PROBLEMS IN IMMENSE FIELDS.

198-199 DURING AN EVENING FLIGHT, A LANDING BALLOON CREATES INTERESTING INTERPLAY OF SHADOWS ON THE HARVESTED WHEAT FIELDS IN THE FRENCH COUNTRYSIDE.

OP WITH EVENING FLIGHTS, IT CAN BE DIFFICULT TO FIND YOUR OWN BALLOON.

NTER NIGHT CAN CATCH YOU UNAWARES.

OTTOM DURING MANY RALLIES THE ORGANIZERS OF THE "NIGHT GLOW" NIGHT-TIME DISPLAY
E PILOTS ACTIVATE THEIR BURNERS TO ILLUMINATE THE BALLOONS.

01 FLYING AT NIGHT IS NEVER EASY BECAUSE THE WIND OFTEN DROPS AND THERE IS A RISK
NG UP ABOVE A FOREST WHEN NIGHT FALLS.

202-203 ONE OF THE
ATTRACTIONS OF THE
SINT-NIKLAAS RALLY IS THE
MINI-BALLOONS DISPLAY. THIS
PICTURE SHOWS A
CONVERSATION BETWEEN TWO
PENGUINS.

sint-niklaas

THE OLDEST MEETING IN EUROPE

It is almost midnight on Sunday, September 7, 2008, when Roy and Annette Sax shake hands with Luc de Wulf, who is a fan of mini hot air balloons. It is the third time in five years that some 15 mini balloons, exact copies of special-shape hot air balloons, have been invited. This was the first innovation introduced into the balloon meeting for special shapes established in 1978, and both the public and the modelmakers are in seventh heaven. In spite of the extremely unfavorable weather conditions, the organizers ensure that their show is a great delight for the numerous spectators and photographers who have come from all over Europe.

Sint-Niklaas may not be one of the great centers of the ballooning world, but it is still proud of its long association with hot air balloons. The first balloon flight took place in Paris in 1783 and only a year later experiments with aerostatic balloons were already happening in Sint-Niklaas. In 1784 Johannes van Goethem, the son of a local goldsmith, inflated the first balloon and ascended from his mother's property near the city center. The balloon rose up to 345 ft (105 m), flew over the great Market Square, and landed in the garden of a house in a neighboring street. It was, however, a further 60 years before the first manned flight took place in Sint-Niklaas. On March 3, 1845, Monsieur Kirch took off from the school courtyard in the very heart of the city. He used the balloon owned by the Antwerp Association and after a flight of approximately 4 miles (6 km) he landed in Belsele. Today, during the meeting, this courtyard is used as a parking place for the pilots.

It was mainly after the Franco-Prussian war of 1870, during which gas balloons had been used very successfully as observation platforms for the artillery, when the balloon regained its popularity. The Belgium and French pilots, such as Jean-Baptiste Glorieux, Camille Dartois, and Adolphe Denys, showed off in a succession of popular fiestas and festivals across the whole of Flanders, thrilling the public with their displays of this invention which finally allowed man to leave the ground and to move through the air. From 1873, during the annual festival held in the first week of July, the people could enjoy regular ascents of balloons from the great square. The Market Square is the second-biggest in Europe after Red Square in Moscow, and was a gift of the countess of Flanders. She commissioned it in 1248 upon the request of Bishop Goswinus, who wanted to build a church there. The countess stipulated that any area of the square which was not to be used for the church could not be used for other purposes, and that it should always be available for the people. Today, many are the balloonists who appreciate her generosity as they ascend from this historic place.

The ballooning tradition was now firmly established and in 1912 several inhabitants founded an association in order to organize air festivals, air baptisms, and flights for scientific experimentation. The association was very successful and it commissioned the construction of two gas balloons. The second, the Waaslander II, was built in 1913, but unfortunately on September 21, 1914, the Belgium army, facing the advance of German troops, requisitioned both balloons. Following the First World War, the aeronautic club did not resume its activity. However, in 1919 the municipal council revived the tradition of balloon flights on Thursday during the July festival.

The flights were again interrupted this time by the Second World War. The city was eventually liberated on September 9, 1944 by British and Polish forces. On the third anniversary of the city's liberation, the mayor at that time, Romain de Vidts, wanted a novel way to commemorate the event. His friend André Sax (descendant of Adolphe Sax, the inventor of the saxophone) proposed reviving the tradition of having balloons ascending from the great square. The idea was discussed with his friend Joseph Van der Straeten, an accomplished balloonist, who agreed immediately. And so the festival was reborn and is today the most historic hot air balloon meeting in the world. In 1948 the event was organized as a race of precision landings, with the participation of five Belgium pilots: Scutenaire, Van Someren, Van der Straeten, Vanden Bemden, and Wallaert. The following year the meeting, which aimed to develop an international reputation for Sint-Niklaas, welcomed the participation of French, Dutch, English, and Swiss pilots. At the 1970 event the modern hot air balloons made their first appearance, including Don Cameron's Golden Eagle, the Petrogaz of François Schaut, and the Planta of Georges Delforge. The success of the modern balloons was so great that in the following years they gradually took over the whole square.

sint-niklaas

After long years of faithful service, in 1972 André Sax and Joseph Van Der Straeten passed the responsibility of the event to Jean Sax. Jean had already obtained his pilot's licence for gas balloons together with his wife Jacqueline, and they both wanted to fly in a hot air balloon. The result was that the Sint-Niklaas meeting became the stage for the first Belgium championship for hot air balloons. In 1978 special-shape balloons arrived at the meeting. The very first was Kermit the Frog owned by the Belgian Patrick Libert. Thanks to the special friendship between Jean Sax, the Forbes family, and Kassia Le Prieur, intendant of Balleroy Castle, almost all the special shapes of the Forbes collection ascended from Sint-Niklaas, including Suleiman, the Motorbike, the Castle, Saint-Mary, the Parrot, and many others. Other special shapes from all over the world included the Polar Bear, the Dinosaur, the Clown, the Bunny, and Santa Claus. These balloons, with their extraordinary shapes and magnificent colors, are today the highlight of the show. They are the balloons that attract the crowds and which the journalists write about in their reviews. In addition to the many special shapes and some 50 hot air balloons there are also six gas balloons, which give the meeting its distinctiveness. Sint-Niklaas is one of the few places in the world where every year people can watch in the inflation of gas balloons in the city center. In the past they needed to be inflated from the city's gas supply, much to the annoyance of the population, but today they are inflated with helium.

From the end of the 1990s, Roy and Annette Sax provided their support for the event, which developed further and further. Nowadays, their daughters Stéphanie and Elisabeth take part and no doubt when the first grandchildren arrive they too will continue the family tradition. Every year the show attracts between 40,000 and 65,000 visitors. The number of spectators depends mainly on the weather conditions. In case of adverse conditions, there are now other attractions as well as the balloons.

206 SINCE 1873 THE GRAND PLACE IN SINT-NIKLAAS HAS HOSTED THE HOT-AIR AND GAS BALLOON FESTIVAL.

206-207 EVERY YEAR THE TOWN OF SINT-NIKLAAS, IN THE FIRST WEEKEND OF SEPTEMBER, ORGANIZES THE TAKEOFF
OF GAS BALLOONS FROM THE TOWN CENTER.

208-209 As with all the big rallies, Sint-Niklaas welcomes crews of special shape balloons, to the great pleasure of the spectators who throng behind the barriers.

209 top With all these animals, at the moment of inflation you might think you were in an enormous zoological park.

209 center A giant parrot looks mischievously at the Cathedral of Saint-Gallen in Switzerland; both were inflated in the Grand Place of Sint-Niklaas.

209 bottom Completely free before flying in the Belgian skies, the American Eagle, emblem of the USA and the parrot, a Brazilian macaw.

210-211 INFLATING 50 BALLOONS IN THE GRAND PLACE OF SINT-NIKLAAS CREATES A FEW SPACE PROBLEMS BUT THE BALLOONS LEAVE IN WAVES SO THAT THEY CAN ALL PARTICIPATE AND THE DISPLAY LASTS LONGER.

211 TOP BEFORE INFLATING THE BALLOONS THE SPECTATORS WATCH A DISPLAY OF REMOTE-CONTROLLED MINI-BALLOONS.

211 BOTTOM VAN GOGH AND THE STRAWBERRY KEEP EACH OTHER COMPANY IN THE GRAND PLACE OF SINT-NIKLAAS.

212-213 *IN SINT-NIKLAAS THERE IS A RETURN TO THE BALLOONING TRADITION WITH THE INFLATION OF GAS BALLOONS THAT STILL USE SAND BAGS AS BALLAST.*

214   *Balloons must be launched quickly in order to avoid the risk of running aground on the roofs of the houses that surround the Grand Place in Sint-Niklaas.*

215   *Taking off from the city center is always an amazing spectacle for the passengers, who can discover historical monuments like this bell-tower in Sint-Niklaas.*

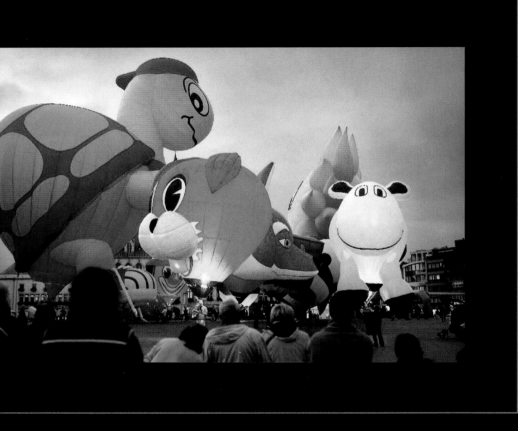

DURING THE FOUR DAYS OF THE SINT-NIKLAAS RALLY, A "NIGHT-GLOW" IS ORGANIZED WITH THE SPECIALLY SHAPED BALLOONS ON THE SATURDAY EVENING.

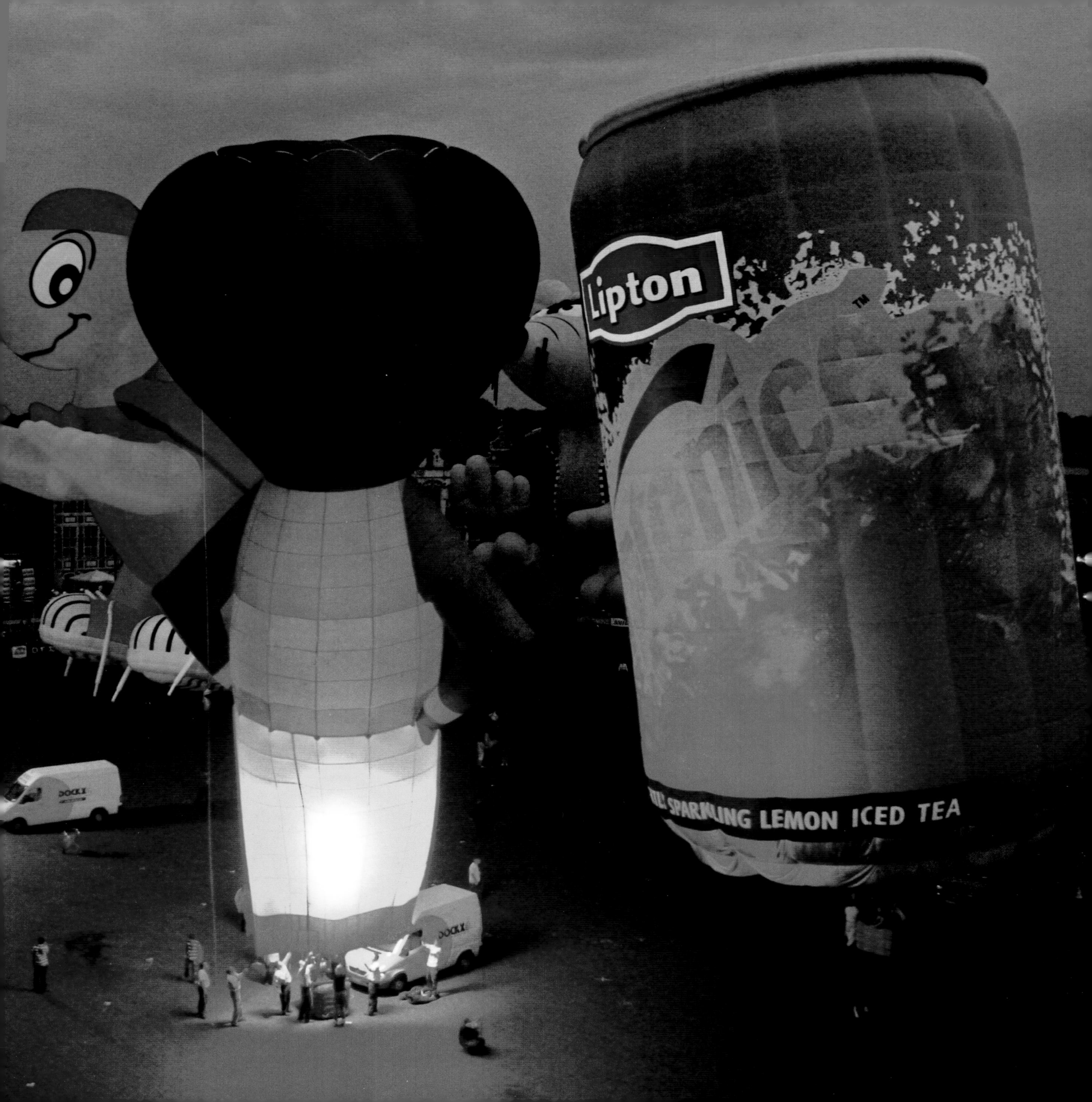
Lipton
SPARKLING LEMON ICED TEA
DOCKX

218-219 UNDER THE EYES OF
THE BALD EAGLE, THE SYMBOL
OF THE USA, THE ENVELOPES
ARE INFLATED DURING THE
BIGGEST MEETING OF HOT AIR
BALLOONS IN THE WORLD, THE
ALBUQUERQUE INTERNATIONAL
BALLOON FIESTA.

albuquerque

TEMPLE TO THE BALLOON

Any pilot who has not participated at least once in the Balloon Festival of Albuquerque cannot know how it feels to ascend into clear blue skies among 800 hot air balloons. It is an incredible experience, so in keeping with the boundless scale of all things American. For nine days, starting on the first week of October, every morning hundreds of colored balloons float over the city. It is not at all surprising that this aerostatic show – a real fiesta for the eyes – is probably the most photographed in the world. Today, Albuquerque is the temple of the hot air balloon and it has become one of the most celebrated events in the world. No other meeting has come close to achieving its size and grandeur. It will celebrate its 40th anniversary in 2012 and will have welcomed by then almost 40,000 hot air balloon pilots.

In Albuquerque everything begins at the end of the night with the flight of the "Dawn Patrol," which are the balloons that fly at night in order to study accurately the meteorological conditions for the following morning. When they give the green light, the balloons are inflated with a deafening noise of ventilators and shouts of the many teams. Once they are ready then begins the magnificent "mass-ascension" of 800 balloons ascending into the sky – a breath-taking spectacle! Unusually, at this event in New Mexico the spectators are allowed to walk around the balloons when they are being inflated and there are no barriers for the thousands of spectators. When a balloon is ready to take off, the "zebras", the launchmasters, so-called because they wear black and white striped uniforms, give the go-ahead accompanied by the cheers of the spectators. A mass-ascent can last almost two hours, because the 800 balloons take off one after another in batches of 10 in order to avoid collisions. Every year some 750,000 people come at Albuquerque to enjoy this remarkable celebration of the hot air balloon.

220 TOP A SYMPATHETIC CHARACTER WILL BE INFLATED FOR THE ASCENSION FROM ALBUQUERQUE.

220 CENTER THIS PIGLET WEARS SUNGLASSES IN ORDER TO PROTECT ITS EYES FROM THE BRIGHT MORNING SUN OF ALBUQUERQUE.

220 BOTTOM THESE SHAPES, WHICH ARE REALLY VERY SPECIAL AND AMONG THE MOST ORIGINAL, ATTRACT THOUSANDS OF SPECTATORS TO THE ALBUQUERQUE FESTIVAL.

220-221 THE TWO BEES ARE SURROUNDED BY SPECTATORS. ONE OF THE UNUSUAL FEATURES OF THE MEETING IS THAT THE PUBLIC HAVE ACCESS TO THE BALLOONS WHILE THEY ARE BEING INFLATED.

222-223 ALBUQUERQUE IS ALSO THE BIGGEST MEETING OF SPECIAL-SHAPED BALLOONS. HERE, THE SWISS COW IS FACING THE DILIGENCE WITHIN THE SPECIAL SHAPE RODEO.

223 TOP LIKE SOMETHING OUT OF JURASSIC PARK THIS DINOSAUR BALLOON HAS BECOME ALMOST AS FAMOUS SPIELBERG'S CREATIONS.

223 CENTER THE SPECIAL SHAPE RODEO USUALLY TAKES PLACE IN THE MIDDLE OF THE WEEK, IN THE AFTERNOON, WHEN THE TRADITIONAL HOT AIR BALLOONS REMAIN ON THE GROUND.

223 BOTTOM A TREE FROM THE AMAZON RAINFOREST WITH A FLOCK OF PARROTS RISES UP AMONG THE OTHER BALLOONS DURING THE SPECIAL SHAPE RODEO.

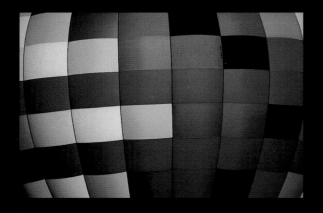

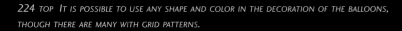

224 TOP IT IS POSSIBLE TO USE ANY SHAPE AND COLOR IN THE DECORATION OF THE BALLOONS, THOUGH THERE ARE MANY WITH GRID PATTERNS.

224 CENTER IN THE DECORATION IT IS ALSO POSSIBLE TO USE SPINDLES, OR GORES, WHICH COMPOUND THE ENVELOPE OF THE BALLOON, OF MUCH OR LESS BIG SIZE AND OF VARIOUS COLOURS.

224 BOTTOM THE "SMILE" OF THE VALVE AT THE MOMENT OF INFLATION.

224-225 EVEN IF THE WHEELS OF A DILIGENCE ARE MADE OF WOOD, IN ALBUQUERQUE THERE ARE INFLATED AS REAL TYRES.

226 top *The diligence is ready to run on the roads of the Far West. It is waiting only for the authorization of the taking-off.*

226 center *An extraordinary spectacle: more than 800 hot air balloons take off in just over an hour from the same field. This is the wonder of Albuquerque.*

226 bottom *A wave of hot air balloons, which seem to be attached to each other, float away over the city of Albuquerque pushed by a gentle wind.*

226-227 *When a balloon is ready to ascend, the "zebras," the launchmasters, so-called because they wear black and white striped uniforms, give the green light to go accompanied by the applause of the spectators.*

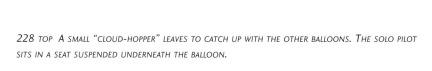

228 TOP A SMALL "CLOUD-HOPPER" LEAVES TO CATCH UP WITH THE OTHER BALLOONS. THE SOLO PILOT SITS IN A SEAT SUSPENDED UNDERNEATH THE BALLOON.

228 BOTTOM THE PILOTS CONTROL EXPERTLY THEIR CRAFT AND CAN PASS WITHIN INCHES OF THE BASKETS OF OTHER BALLOONS.

228-229 ALTHOUGH THERE ARE OFTEN HUNDREDS OF BALLOONS IN THE SKY OVER NEW MEXICO, THERE ARE NO COLLISIONS THANKS TO THE SKILL OF THE PILOTS.

230-231 THE ASCENT OF THE SPECIAL SHAPES IS PERHAPS THE MOST POPULAR EVENT WITH THE SPECTATORS, WHO GATHER IN HUGE CROWDS TO WATCH.

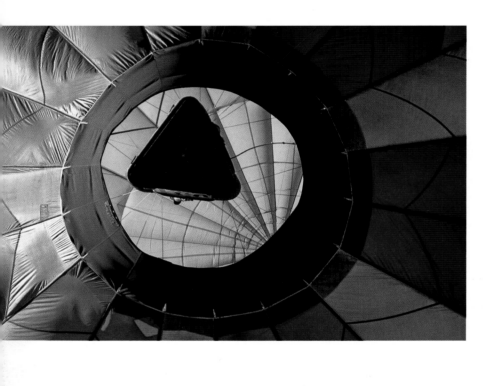

232 *This basket, made by the American manufacturer FireFly, is remarkable. It is triangular and made of steel.*

232-233 *American balloons have at the base of the envelope a kind of skirt (designed by Raven Industries), while in Europe the lower extremities of the balloon are finished with a fabric triangle called scoop.*

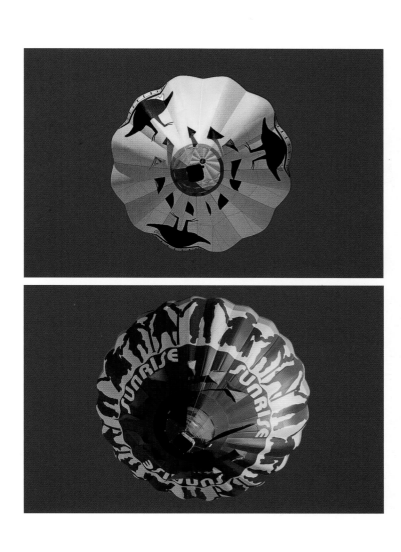

234-235 THE DESIGNERS OF HOT AIR BALLOONS ARE CLEARLY ENCOURAGED TO EXPRESS THEMSELVES
AS IMAGINATIVELY AS THEY WISH IN THE DEOCRATION OF THESE SPECTACULAR CRAFT.

235 IT IS POSSIBLE TO DECORATE A BALLOON IN SUCH A WAY THAT WHEN IT RISES INTO THE SKY ITS
DESIGN, BRAND ICON, OR SLOGAN CAN BE SEEN EASILY FROM THE GROUND.

236-237 AMERICANS DELIGHT IN DECORATING THEIR BALLOONS WITH STARS, NO DOUBT INSPIRED BY THEIR NATIONAL FLAG.

237 A GROUP OF AMERICAN BALLOONS IN THE SKY OVER ALBUQUERQUE, EASILY RECOGNIZABLE BY THE COLORS AND DESIGN OF THEIR DECORATION.

238-239 THE DISTANCE BETWEEN BALLOONS CAN BE SO SMALL THAT IT IS POSSIBLE FOR ONE CREW TO TALK TO ANOTHER.

240 TOP OFTEN A PILOT ENJOYS GETTING AS CLOSE AS HE CAN TO WATER FOR THE GREAT PLEASURE AND EXCITEMENT OF THE PASSENGERS.

240 BOTTOM SOME PILOTS DECIDE TO DANGLE THEIR FEET IN A RIVER.

240-241 ONE OF AMERICA'S BIGGEST RIVERS, THE LEGENDARY RIO GRANDE, FLOWS THROUGH ALBUQUERQUE AND THE BALLOONS OFTEN FLOAT OVER THIS RIVER WHICH HAS FEATURED IN MANY WESTERNS.

242 top Crossing the Rio Grande in a balloon is a magnificent way to pass from one riverbank to the other, with a short stop on the island in the middle.

242 bottom After having crossed the Rio Grande, the pilots then head out into the desert of New Mexico.

242-243 Flying over the mighty Rio Grande is a significant moment, particularly for the foreign pilots who have never seen the river before.

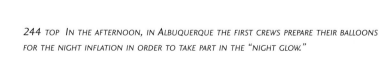

244 TOP IN THE AFTERNOON, IN ALBUQUERQUE THE FIRST CREWS PREPARE THEIR BALLOONS FOR THE NIGHT INFLATION IN ORDER TO TAKE PART IN THE "NIGHT GLOW."

244 CENTER THE FLAMES OF THE BURNERS ILLUMINATE THE BALLOONS LIKE GIANT LANTERNS.

244 BOTTOM THE FLAME WARMS UP THE AIR IN THE ENVELOPE. THE BURNER IS ACTIVATED AND THE BALLOON IS READY FOR THE "NIGHT GLOW."

244-245 IN ORDER TO BE READY FOR THE "NIGHT GLOW," THE PILOTS ACTIVATE THE BURNERS AT SUNSET.

246-247 TODAY, ALBUQUERQUE WELCOMES ALMOST 80 SPECIAL-SHAPED BALLOONS AND THE "NIGHT GLOW" IS ALWAYS AN ENORMOUS SUCCESS WITH THE PUBLIC. THEY ARRIVE IN THEIR THOUSANDS AS EVENING FALLS TO WATCH THIS MAGICAL SHOW.

247 EVERY NIGHT OF THE BALLOON FESTIVAL, NO MATTER IF THERE ARE SPECIAL SHAPES OR JUST THE TRADITIONAL BALLOONS, HUGE CROWDS ENJOY THE "NIGHT GLOWS." AS THE BALLOONS ARE ILLUMINATED ONE BY ONE THEY ARE ALWAYS GREETED BY GREAT CHEERS AND APPLAUSE IN AN ATMOSPHERE OF DELIGHTED CELEBRATION.

248-249 DAY OR NIGHT, THE PUBLIC CAN GET CLOSE TO THE HOT AIR BALLOONS AND TRULY PARTICIPATE IN THIS GREAT BALLOON EXTRAVAGANZA. THIS ONLY HAPPENS AT ALBUQUERQUE. AT EVENTS IN THE REST OF THE WORLD SPECTATORS ARE KEPT BEHIND BARRIERS.

The special shapes

  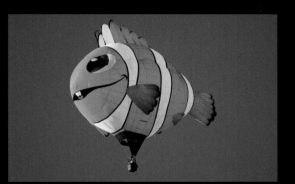

the great attraction of the rallies

THE RULE OF THE IMAGINATION

Hot air balloons make us smile and dream, especially those with unusual and imaginative shapes which provide such incomparable spectacles at every take-off. They have been produced in every imaginable shape, even the most bizarre, and the sight of these large objects in the sky is magical. Think of the Virgin aircrafts or the bagpipe player owned by Muir Moffat, which is almost 230 ft (70 m) in height, or you may have glimpsed a sphinx, a turtle, a cock, a cathedral, or even a Harley-Davidson.

However, these special shapes are usually seen only rarely, due to how diffcult they are to steer and the expense of manufacturing them. It is simply more difficult to manufacture, inflate, and control balloons that have an unusual shape compared to the traditional hot air balloon. Also, they require a significant number of additional support staff, because the envelopes are much heavier than the ordinary ones, even if they have the same volume. Furthermore, the pilot of such a balloon must be very experienced.

One of the first manufacturers of balloons to create special shapes was the English engineer Don Cameron, who realized earlier than most other people the potential value of such airships. In 1975, he designed the Golly III, the first special-shaped balloon, which was commissioned by Robertson's, the preserve manufacturer, who had a golliwog as a mascot, and a balloon in the shape of a pair of Levi's jeans. Originally, the Levi's envelope was intended to fly with two baskets, one under each leg, in order to keep the perfect symmetry of a pair of jeans, however, the tests did not appear very convincing and finally the jeans flew with a single basket, and the other leg was closed at the base and filled only with cold air. So far more than 300 special-shaped envelopes have been manufactured by the Cameron Balloons Company of Bristol, including a dragon, a space shuttle, every kind of animal, preserve jars, houses, and bottles.

Don Cameron wished to push the limits of balloon manufacturing as far as possible, and the special-shaped envelopes are partly the result of this ambition. Every pilot dreams of flying a special-shaped envelope, as it represents a new form of air advertising. People will always look at a hot air balloon flying past and so a special-shaped envelope causes even more of a commotion on the ground. One thing that always makes people wonder is how those unusual shapes can fly: a floating house seems to defy gravity.

However, following on from the first special-shaped balloons, particularly developing on from Golly III flown in 1976 at the Bristol Balloon Fiesta, Don Cameron's designs evolved into more and more complex models. By now customers were aware that the limit to the realization of their dreams was dictated only by the limits of their imagination.

Due to the high costs, normally these balloon are not owned by individuals, except if they are extremely rich and wish to indulge themselves, but by companies that have their balloons flown by professional pilots and use them only to advertise, because often such craft do not have the authorization to carry passengers. Such balloons are great favourites at festivals. However, as they are so expensive to maintain and require a significant number of ground staff when being inflated, they may not appear at all balloon festivals. Nevertheless, nowadays some organizations run meetings just for special-shaped balloons, such as the

254 Muir Muffat's
balloon, a Scottish bagpipe
player which is 230 ft
(70 m) high, always makes
a great impression
at Château-d'Oex.

world-famous Albuquerque International Balloon Fiesta. In 1989, Scott Appelman, one of the organizers of this fiesta, got the idea to inlcude this new type of balloon, but he had difficulties getting the approval of the board of directors of his company. A factor in Scott Appelman's favor was his friendship with Mark Sullivan, who knew many of the pilots of the special-shaped balloons and also their owners, and he was able to invite them. A further problem to be overcome was the great expense of running such an event. Where would the funding come from? However, in the end the Appelman's proposal was accepted and the fiesta was named Special Shape Rodeo.

With the specially shaped balloons, the organizers hope not only to attract visitors but also to promote the loyalty of the public with an extraordinary spectacle. Until then, special shapes, which are a completely new type of balloon, had never participated at the Albuquerque Rally. The committee decided to have them take off on Thursday and Friday afternoon, because in Albuquerque there are usually no afternoon flights. Fortunately, in 1989 the organizers were blessed with extraordinary meteorological conditions, so much so that the two mass takeoff operations were completed without any problems, except for the huge traffic jams caused by the large number of spectators who wanted to see the spectacle. Moreover, it was a première: 28 special shapes took part in this first edition of the competition. The "Special Shapes Rodeo" has become increasingly important over the years; in 1996 the organizers beat their own record with 106 balloons participating. As well as being the biggest balloon meeting in the world today, Albuquerque is also the largest existing special shapes rodeo.

Over the years, organizers decided to introduce a "night glow" show exclusively for special shapes, which they called "Glowdeo." The night-time inflation of the balloons has always met with huge success.

Thanks to the increasing success of the special shapes, almost 750,000 spectators attend the 10 days of aerostatic displays and spectacles at this great balloon festival.

Other rallies followed suit and included the special shapes balloons in their program: Bristol welcomes almost 25 specially shaped balloons. The first takeoff of the rally is on the Thursday evening with these balloons. The public rushes en masse to applaud every single takeoff: a jaguar, a bagpipe player, a house with smoke coming out of the chimney, a strawberry – something to cater for all tastes. There is also something for all photographers: flashes pop everywhere. More than 100,000 spectators witness this "close encounter of the third kind."

In Canada, the International Balloon Festival of Saint-Jean-sur-Richelieu is held in the middle of August. Here, too, the special shapes ensure "a magic flight." Since 2005, for nine days, people come to admire up to two flights of special-shaped hot air balloons every day, depending on the weather conditions. The event now welcomes 115 balloons and among these there are about 15 special-shaped ones. Adults and children remain fascinated by balloons shaped like a panda, a turtle, a cockerel, a pirate, a monkey's head, or a bear, not to mention a beaver, a pink elephant, a pair of bees, as well as the angelic and diabolic duo Angel and Burnie the Devil. There are also the usual visitors, Piko, Titty, and the giant daisy, Miss Daisy.

As already mentioned, these fantastical, special-shaped balloons are appreciated not only by the crowds for the delightful and wonderful spectacle they provide, but also by the pilots for the challenge and fun of flying them. It is certain that without the sponsors, who are modestly known as godparents, these balloons would never have been created. However, although expensive to make and fly, their image is always associated with cheerfulness and fancifulness, evoked by the dream-like sight of such unusual objects floating across a clear-blue sky over the countryside or a city.

The special shapes

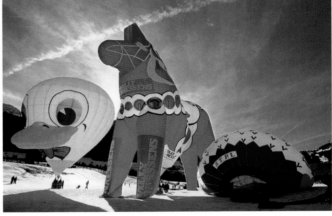

256-257 A SWISS CAT IS HUNTING A MOUSE AT THE CHÂTEAU-D'OEX MEETING. THE SPECIAL-SHAPED BALLOONS, WHICH ASCEND ON SATURDAY AND SUNDAY AT NOON, ATTRACT HUGE CROWDS EVERY YEAR.

257 TOP A RED HEART SYMBOLIZES THE PASSION FOR BALLOONS DURING THE MEETING "BALLOONS IN LOVE" IN CARPINETI, ITALY.

257 CENTER THE BELGIAN TURTLE MISTER BUP IS ALWAYS ONE OF THE MOST POPULAR BALLOONS WITH THE YOUNGER SPECTATORS.

257 BOTTOM A HORSE AND A DUCK: PEOPLE RECALL THE FAIRYTALES OF LA FONTAINE, ESPECIALLY WHEN THEY LOOK AT THE FRENCH COCK, WHILE IT IS INFLATED FOR THE MEETING IN CHÂTEAU-D'OEX, SWITZERLAND.

258 and 258-259 Bibendum, the Michelin Man, at Château-d'Oex is a real monster in comparison to the other balloons. Just inflating this balloon is a show in itself. The Michelin balloons, there are 12 in total all of different dimensions and shapes, were made for the centenary of Bibendum. They have been all over the world, participating in many different events, such as this one at Château-d'Oex, Switzerland, in 1998.

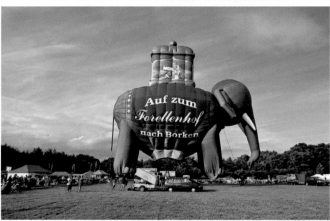

260 TOP THE COCA-COLA BOTTLE AS IT LANDS.

260 CENTER AMONG SEVERAL OTHER BOTTLES WHICH HAVE INSPIRED SPECIAL-SHAPED BALLOONS,
THE ONE OF JÄGERMEISTER DEFLATES DURING A GERMAN MEETING.

260 BOTTOM THIS WONDERFULLY REALISTIC ELEPHANT HOT AIR BALLOON HAS AN ALMOST
SURREAL QUALITY.

260-261 THE COCA-COLA BOTTLE LAID DOWN AFTER LANDING. ONCE DEFLATED THE ENVELOPE HAS
TO BE FOLDED UP, WHICH CAN BE A DIFFICULT TASK WITH THE SPECIAL-SHAPED BALLOONS.

262-263 THE DESIGNS OF THE SPECIAL-SHAPED BALLOONS HAVE BEEN INSPIRED BY OTHER MODES OF TRANSPORT. HERE WE CAN SEE A STEAM LOCOMOTIVE OF THE ORIENT EXPRESS, WITH A GERMAN PILOT AT THE BURNER.

263 TOP VARIOUS AIR COMPANIES HAVE SPONSORED BALLOONS IN ORDER TO USE THEM FOR ADVERTISING AND MARKETING.

263 BOTTOM EVEN COMPANIES INVOLVED IN THE PALLET BUSINESS HAVE LAUNCHED THEIR OWN HOT AIR BALLOON.

264 THIS ENORMOUS CHURCH, THE SAINT-GALLEN CATHEDRAL, WITH TOWERS THAT WOBBLE WHENEVER THE WIND GETS STRONGER, IS IN THE SWISS SKIES.

264-265 A BUNNY COMES NEARER TO BERLIN'S BRANDENBURG GATE, WHICH IS SO REALISTIC THAT IT SEEMS TO BE A REAL MONUMENT AND NOT A HOT AIR BALLOON.

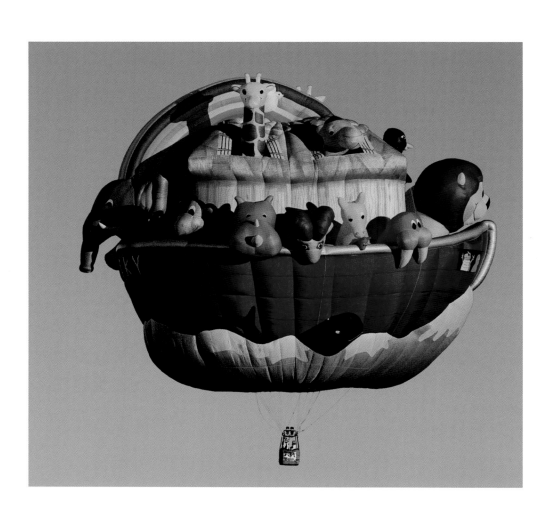

266 AND 266-267 IN THE SKY OVER ALBUQUERQUE AN ENORMOUS NOAH'S ARK FILLED WITH ANIMALS FLOATS AWAY, PUSHED BY THE WIND.

268-269 IMPRESSIVE AND YET HORRIBLE, IT IS VERY DIFFICULT TO IDENTIFY THIS AS A LION AS IT SHOULD BE MAJESTIC AS BEFITTING THE KING OF THE BEASTS. IT IS NOT A GREAT DESIGN, BUT IT DOES FLY.

270 *FOOD AND DRINK ARE NOT FORGOTTEN: A PUMPKIN TO CELEBRATE HALLOWEEN (TOP LEFT); A BEER MUG IN THE SKY OVER CHÂTEAU-D'OEX (TOP RIGHT); A TEMPTING BIRTHDAY CAKE — WHOSE AMERICAN PILOT IS OFTEN INVITED TO CELEBRATE THE 20TH OR THE 30TH ANNIVERSARY OF MEETINGS, AS HERE IN CHAMBLEY, FRANCE (BOTTOM LEFT); AN ICE-CREAM CONE AMONG THE AUSTRIAN MOUNTAINS COVERED WITH SNOW (BOTTOM RIGHT).*

271 *THE BELGIANS AND THE GERMANS ADORE BEER AND THEIR BALLOONS OFTEN REFLECT THIS PASSION. A BEER TASTING AFTER LANDING IS GUARANTEED.*

272 TOP PUBLICITY FOR A DAIRY INDUSTRY OF NEW MEXICO: A NICE COW, WHICH IS ALWAYS WELCOMED AT ALBUQUERQUE.

272 CENTER ANIMALS ARE POPULAR DESIGNS FOR SPECIAL-SHAPED BALLOONS, AND THIS RABBIT IS A PARTICULAR FAVORITE WITH CHILDREN.

272 BOTTOM THIS GERMAN LITTLE MOUSE PARTICIPATES IN MANY MEETINGS.

272-273 THE SPECIAL SHAPE RODEO AT THE ALBUQUERQUE FESTIVAL HAS ANIMALS OF EVERY KIND, SUCH AS THIS PIGLET-GANGSTER.

274-275 THE BALLOON MANUFACTURERS NEED TO HAVE A GREAT DEAL OF IMAGINATION WHEN CREATING SPECIAL SHAPES, AND ALSO A CLIENT WHO WANTS TO HAVE AN ORDINARY BALLOON TRANSFORMED INTO SOMETHING WHIMSICAL AND FANTASTIC.

275 JUST ARMS, LEGS, AND A NICE FACE AND THERE IS A VERY SIMPLE BUT EFFECTIVE SPECIAL-SHAPED BALLOON, WHICH IS ABLE TO FLY PERFECTLY.

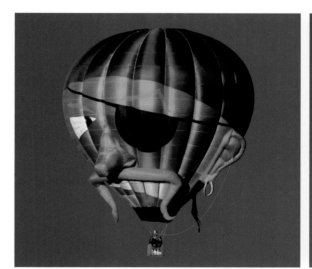

276-277 FANTASY CHARACTERS AND THE COMIC-BOOK HEROES ARE ALWAYS POPULAR AND HAVE INSPIRED MANY BALLOONS, SUCH AS THIS WITCH, WHICH TAKES OFF EVERY YEAR TO CELEBRATE HALLOWEEN IN THE USA.

277 TOP A PURELY IMAGINARY CHARACTER FLIES IN THE SKY OVER ALBUQUERQUE.

277 BOTTOM MANY BALLOONS, MAINLY IN THE USA, HAVE CORSAIR OR PIRATE DESIGNS WITH A SKULL AND CROSSBONES ON THE ENVELOPE.

278 AND 279 THE MONSTERS SHOULD BE FRIGHTENING, BUT AS FIERCE-LOOKING AS THEY ARE THEY ALWAYS DELIGHT THE SPECTATORS. EVERY KIND OF CREATURE YOU CAN IMAGINE HAS BEEN PRODUCED, FROM MYTHICAL BEASTS TO JUST PLAIN TERRIFYING ONES! HOWEVER, THERE ARE ALSO CUTE MONSTERS WHICH MAKE PEOPLE SMILE.

 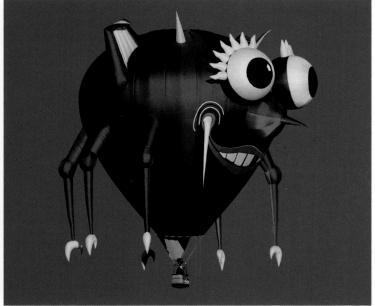

280 LEFT A TREE FLOATS OVER ALBUQUERQUE. A DELIGHTFUL AND ORIGINAL BALLOON.

280 RIGHT AN OCTOPUS WITH GOOFY EYES IS ONLY ONE OF VARIOUS OTHER MARINE CREATURES YOU CAN FIND IN THE SKY.

281 THIS AMERICAN MONSTER IS KNOWN THROUGHOUT THE WORLD AND HAS VISITED EUROPE ON MANY OCCASIONS, INCLUDING THE CHÂTEAU-D'OEX MEETING, THE FRANÇOIS IER TROPHY, AND THE BIENNIAL OF BALLOONING AT CHAMBLEY.

282 TOP MANY SPECIAL-SHAPED HOT AIR BALLOONS NATURALLY HAVE BEEN INSPIRED BY BIRDS, WHETHER STYLIZED OR REALISTICALLY, SUCH
AS THIS PARROT (LEFT), A BRAZILIAN ARA, THE PEACOCK (CENTER) FROM THE NETHERLANDS, OR THE FRENCH COCK (RIGHT), WHICH
IS THE MASCOT OF THE "BALLOONING ADVENTURES" ASSOCIATION AND IS IN THE BLUE, WHITE, AND RED COLORS OF THE FRENCH FLAG.

282 BOTTOM AS TWO LITTLE BROTHERS, THESE TWO GERMAN PINGUINS HAVE A VERY SYMPHATIC EXPRESSION.

282-283 FROM TIME IMMEMORIAL CHILDREN HAVE BEEN TOLD, ESPECIALLY IN ALSACE, FRANCE, THAT IT IS THE STORKS THAT BRING BABIES.
A MYTH MADE REAL IN THE WORLD OF HOT AIR BALLOONS.

284 WONDERFUL CREATURES FROM THE OCEANS ARE ALSO POPULAR DESIGNS, SUCH AS THIS SUPERB OCTOPUS, WHICH CARRIES AN ENTIRE COLONY OF SEA ANIMALS — STARFISHES, SEAHORSES, AND EVEN DOLPHINS.

285 ON THE OTHER HAND, THE CLOWN FISH WALLY IN THE SKY OVER ALBUQUERQUE IS NOT HIDING ... NOT EVEN IN ITS ANEMONE. THE COLORS ARE WONDERFUL AND IT IS A VERY GOOD LIKENESS TO THE REAL ONE.

286-287 THIS SCARECROW WITH A SURPRISED EXPRESSION SEEMS TO BE ASTONISHED TO BE ENCOUNTERING OTHER HOT AIR BALLOONS IN THE ALBUQUERQUE SKIES THAT ARE DIFFERENT FROM THE SPECIAL-SHAPED ONES.

288-289 THE NOAH'S ARK FLIES TOWARDS THIS MAGNIFICIENT FISH.

289 A SUNFLOWER IS WINKING TO THE LITTLE AMERICAN MONK IN THE VAST CLEAR AMERICAN SKIES.

290 In Jean de La Fontaine's story the frog that wanted to become as big as a buffalo could not imagine that its dream would be realized as a hot air balloon.

291 Mister Bup, the cute turtle belonging to Lenny and Julie Cant, who have traveled around the world with their delightful friend.

292-293 LILLY AND JOEY, THE LITTLE AMERICAN BEES FROM ARIZONA, HAVE BEEN
AWARDED FOUR TIMES THE AUDIENCE PRIZE OF THE ALBUQUERQUE INTERNATIONAL
BALLOON FIESTA.

293 THE ONLY SPECIAL-SHAPED BALLOONS THAT FLY IN TANDEM, THE BEES SUPRISE
AND DELIGHT SPECTATORS FROM ALL OVER THE WORLD.

294 *In the insect world flying is absolutely normal, but it could be a nasty wasp which will try to sting you, that is flying around.*

295 *The charming ladybird Lady Bug designed in Brazil is owned by a pilot from Arizona. It was first seen in September 2008 at Gatineau, Canada.*

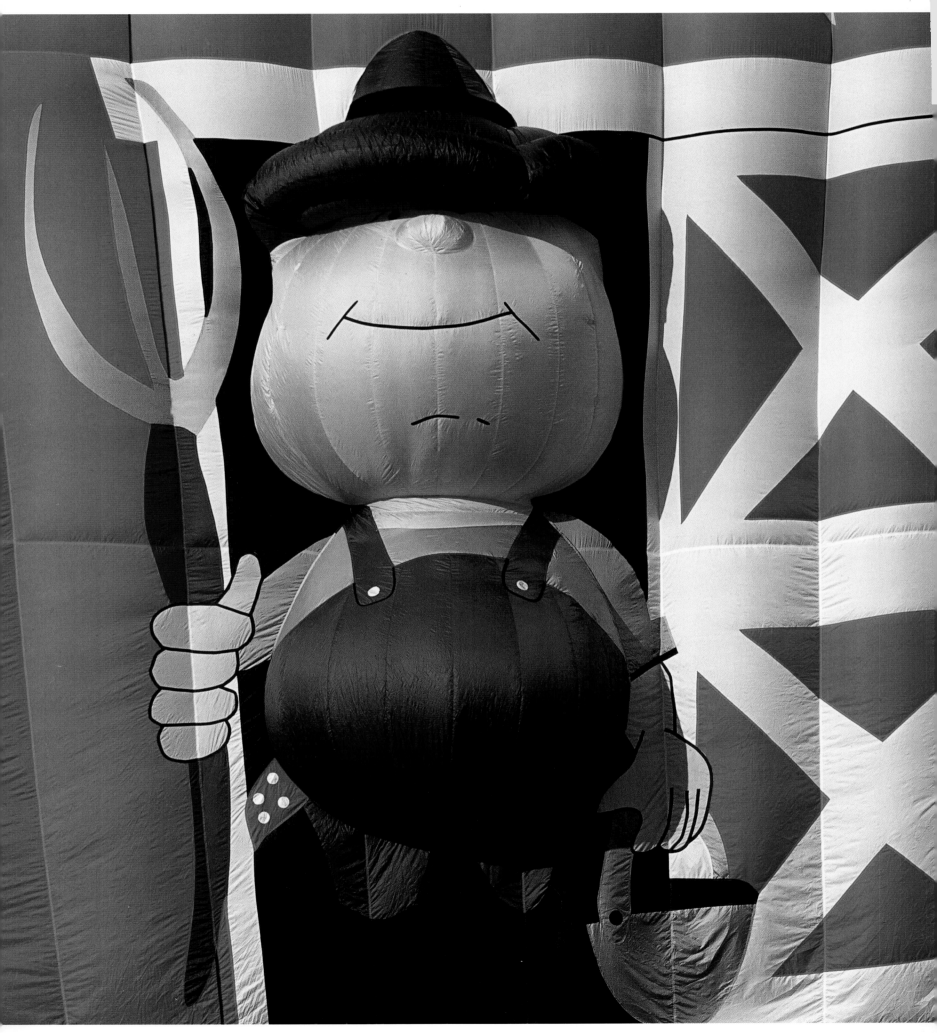

296-297 NUMEROUS FARM ANIMALS CAN ALSO BE SEEN AS SPECIAL-SHAPED BALLOONS. HERE IS A FARMER SUPERVISING HIS BARNYARD.

297 TOP THIS SMALL FARM OF THE BIG AMERICAN VALLEYS IS SUPRIZING FURTHER MANY FARMERS WORKING ON THE GROUND.

297 BOTTOM SEEN UP CLOSE THE DESIGN FOR THE FRENCH COCK SEEMS TO BE TAKEN FROM A COMIC.

298-299 THE SPECIAL SHAPE RODEO AT ALBUQUERQUE REMAINS THE MOST FAMOUS SPECIAL-SHAPED BALLOON MEETING IN THE WORLD. IN 2008 IT WELCOMED 120 SPECIAL SHAPES AND IN 2009 IT CELEBRATE ITS 20TH ANNIVERSARY.

GLOSSARY

Aircraft: According to the International Aeronautics Federation, aircraft are divided into aerostats, which are lighter than air, and aerodynes, which are heavier than air. The aerostats navigate on the air currents, the so-called "jet streams," or float, while the aerodynes fly.

Aeroplane: An aeroplane is supported by its planes, namely by means of its wings. An aerostat instead remains stable in the air.

Aerostat: An envelope, inflated with a gas, which is lighter than air, that is pushed by the wind and is not dirigible.

Airplane: In French the term *aéroplane* was used to describe military machines until the aviation minister decided to call them *avions* in homage of Clément Ader, who had named his first airplanes "Avion 1 - Eole", "Avion 2 – Zéphir," and "Avion 3 - Aquilon". *Avion* comes from the Latin word *avis*, meaning a bird, and Aeolus, Zephyr, and Aquilon, which are names of winds. Aeolus was the god of the winds.

Ballast: This consists of sand bags fixed on the external side of the basket and is only used in gas balloons. In order to ascend, sand bags are released, and in order to descend the valve is opened. A hot-air balloon does not carry any ballast, because it uses warm air to achieve altitude.

Basket: An open or pressurized capsule.

Braked flight: A balloon is fixed to a big rope so that it can float but not fly away. The opposite of this is a "free flight," when the balloon is able to move with the air currents.

Cylinder: The more technical term for a propane container which may also be known as a "tank."

Envelope: Also known as a skin or sail. The envelope of a hot-air balloon is made of nylon with a weight of 60 gr/m^2. It should not be warmed up to more than 248°F (120°C).

Gas balloon: A gas balloon is an aerostat. Often it seems to be very big, however, this is due to the distance between the basket and the balloon. Actually, the envelope is much smaller than the one used for a hot-air balloon, because the ascending force of a gas, such as helium or hydrogen, is greater than that of hot air. A gas balloon consists of two main components: an envelope of water-resistant, rubberized canvas, which keeps the gas inside, and a basket of steel and rattan. It is also known as a *charlière*, for its inventor Jacques Charles, or, more rarely, as a *robertine* for its original constructors the Robert brothers.

GPS: Global Positioning System is a satellite navigation system using information from 26 satellites. The satellites transmit a constant radio signal. By calculating the duration of a signal from a satellite, as well as the time which is required for its arrival to the receiving device, it is possible to calculate the distance that separates the satellite from the receiver. This system enables people to establish location, course, and direction.

Helium: An inert and harmless gas, which is lighter than the air. It is often used to inflate toy balloons. It is used for the rosier balloons and the gas balloons, and it is much expencive than the hydrogen.

Hooks: The hooks are used to connect the basket's ropes to the envelope ropes.

Hot air: Electricity was a recent discovery in 1783 and the Montgolfier brothers were convinced that their invention could fly thanks to an electric phenomenon caused by the smoke! It was a physicist from Geneva, Horace Bénédict de Saussure, who, in his memoirs which he dedicated to the brothers, proved that it was the effect of the hot air and not electricity that made the balloons fly.

Hot-air balloon: An aerostat.

Hydrogen: A gas that is lighter than air, highly inflammable and so more dangerous than helium.

Inflation: The inflation of a hot-air balloon is the first operation carried out prior to an ascent. First, the envelope is spread on the ground, then it is fixed to the basket, which is leaning on its side. A small ventilator blows cold air into the balloon. When the envelope is inflated by two-thirds, the burner is turned on, which warms up the air inside.

Jet stream: Air currents discovered by pilots in the Second World War. The jet stream is a very fast air current some hundreds of miles wide but only a few miles deep, generally situated in the tropopause at 6–9 miles (10–15 km) above the Earth's surface. These currents blow from west to east due to the rotation of the Earth. The speed of the winds inside the currents can be about 125–190 mph (200–300 km/h), but they can reach up to 250 mph (400 km/h). The jet streams have been used by balloonists in the their attempts to fly around the world, in particular Bertrand Piccard and Brian Jones.

Leading flame: In each burner is permanently turned on a leading flame.

Load panel: The burner is fixed on a platform of stainless steel, the basket is hung from it, and the cables of the envelope are fixed to the platform by means of hooks. The loading platform is an essential component of both hot-air balloons and gas balloons. On the gas balloons it connects the basket and the net.

Maneuver rope: This is a rope, fixed on a crown ring, located on the top of the balloon. It does not have any function during the flight, but during the inflation a team member holds onto it and tightens it as the envelope extends. During the deflation, it enables the envelope to be brought to the ground. During the flight, the rope hangs from the envelope and and is tied to the loading platform or the burner frame.

Manometer: A measurement device, mounted on the burner, that indicates in bars the pressure of the propane arriving to the burner.

Marker: The marker is used to "mark" during races. It is a nylon bag full of sand with a yard-long tag on which is written the number of the competitor.

Meeting: A hot-air balloon meeting, also known as Montgolfiades.

Mouth: The opening at the base of a hot-air balloon, which lets the burner's flames pass through.

Nitrogen: In order to work properly, the burner needs a minimum pressure of 4 bars. At lower temperatures the propane remains liquid and the pressure decreases. In order to compensate for this pressure decrease, nitrogen is injected to pressurize the cylinders and so provide for the right pressure of the propane.

On-board instruments: Compasses, barometer, altimeter, GPS – all the devices that allow pilots to establish their position and direction.

Parachute: The top of the envelope, which is open, is plugged from the inner side by a movable circular panel called the "parachute" or valve. Under the pressure of the hot air the valve is pushed to the extremity of the envelope and so keeps it closed.

Red rope: The rope that comes out from the inner part of the balloon and which regulates the opening of the parachute valve.

Refuelling: The filling of the propane cylinders.

Spindles (strips): The manufacturing techniques of envelopes is the same for all hot-air balloon manufacturers. The vertical spindles, between 8 and 32, divided in panels, are assembled together by means of straps. The higher the number of spindles, the smoother the balloon, on the opposite of the balloon made of eight spindles, which is well-shaped.

Valve: The spindles leave an opening at the top of the hot-air balloon. On each spindle there are some Velcro strips in order to facilitate the correct deployment of the valve at the moment of the inflation. In flight, the push of the hot air forces the valve against the envelope. The valve is activated by the pilot by pulling the appropriate rope.

Ventilator: The ventilator is used to inflate the envelope with cold air. Once inflated on the ground, the pilot then warms up the cold air and the balloon straightens and rises up thanks to the effect of the hot air.

There are no age limits for enjoying a flight in a hot-air balloon, however, those under 4 ft (1 m 20 cm) run the risk of not being able to appreciate the view as they won't be able to see over the side of the basket.

BIBLIOGRAPHY

Les Ballons du futur, by Pierre Balaskovic and François Moizard, (May 1994) editions "ACE éditeur"

Romantic Ballooning, Jean-Marc Culas, (1988) editions Seeger Druck und Verlag

Le temps des ballons, art et histoire, Musée de l'air et de l'espace, Le Bourget (1994) Editions de la Martinière

Bulles d'Atmosphère, (The ships in the sky) by Marco Majrani, (1993), Pix Art Edizioni

200 ans de montgolfières, Ballons à gaz et dirigeables, Pierre Léotard, (1983) editions Solar-Paris

Ballons, la plus noble conquête de l'air, (December 1992), Claude Henry Laval, Philippe Maille, editions Jean-Pierre Taillandier.

Aventures et exploits en montgolfières, (1983) Philippe

Buron Pilâtre, editions ACLA.

Biennale mondiale de l'aérostation, le rendez-vous des cinq continents (1991) Philippe Buron-Pilâtre, editions GPC

Montgolfière, la passion, (1989) by Bernard Brattières and Jean-Luc Franco, editions Syros.

Il mondo delle mongolfiere, Antonio Biasioli, (2002) editions Sport Balloon edizioni

Around the World in 20 Days: The Story of Our History-Making Balloon Flight (November 1999), Bertrand Piccard and Brian Jones, John Wiley and Sons Ltd

Le rêve d'Icare, (1985), Urs Scheidegger, editions Avanti

Château-d'Oex, Atmosphère-atmosphère, (October 1997), Anouk Ortlieb, Tourist Office Editions, Château-d'Oex.

Les Ballons montés (1992) Gérard Lhéritier, editions Valeur Philatélique

Ballooning - Handbook (1980) Don Cameron editions Pelham Books

Le pilotage des montgolfières, editions Cepadues

Une trace sand le ciel (2005), Bertand Piccard, Éditions Favre SA, Lausanne-Paris

By Jean Becker:

Le Spitzberg en montgolfières, (November 1988) editions France Région

Carnets de vols en Laponie, (September 2002) editions Impressions graphiques

INDEX

PHOTO CREDITS

All photographs are by Roberto Magni and Daniela Comi except the following:

Pages 4-5 Jean Becker

Pages 10-11 Solar Impulse/Stéphane Gros

Pages 14-15, 16 left, 16 right, 17 Jean Becker

Page 18 courtesy of Parmigiani Fleurier

Pages 19, 20 left, 20 right Jean Becker

Page 21 courtesy of Parmigiani Fleurier

Page 31 right courtesy of Tibor Balint, Jet Propulsion Laboratory, NASA

Page 32 Marc Charmet/The Art Archive

Page 33 Hulton Archive/Getty Images

Pages 34, 36 The Bridgeman Art Library/Archivi Alinari, Firenze

Page 35 The Bridgeman Art Library/Getty Images

Page 37 top Rischgitz/Getty Images

Page 37 bottom The Bridgeman Art Library/Getty Images

Page 38 Gianni Dagli Orti/The Art Archive

Pages 38-39 Ann Ronan Picture Library/Photos12.com

Pages 40 top, 40 bottom The Bridgeman Art Library/Archivi Alinari, Firenze

Page 41 The Bridgeman Art Library/Getty Images

Pages 42, 43 The Bridgeman Art Library/Archivi Alinari, Firenze

Pages 44, 45 PhotoserviceElecta/AKG Images

Pages 46 The Bridgeman Art Library/Archivi Alinari, Firenze

Page 47 The Bridgeman Art Library/Getty Images

Pages 48-49 Harper Collins Publishers/The Art Archive

Page 49 Roger Viollet/Archivi Alinari, Firenze

Pages 50-51 Stefano Bianchetti/Corbis

Page 51 Marc Charmet/The Art Archive

Page 52 top Eileen Tweedy/The Art Archive

Page 52 bottom Harper Collins Publishers/The Art Archive

Pages 52-53, 54 top, 54 bottom The Bridgeman Art Library/Getty Images

Page 55 courtesy of the Library of Congress, Prints and Photographs Division, LC-DIG-ppmsca-02337

Page 56 The Bridgeman Art Library/Archivi Alinari, Firenze

Page 57 Gianni Dagli Orti/The Art Archive

Page 58 Rue des Archives

Pages 58-59 The Bridgeman Art Library/Archivi Alinari, Firenze

Pages 60-61 The Bridgeman Art Library/Getty Images

Page 61 Marc Charmet/The Art Archive

Page 62 Alfredo Dagli Orti/The Art Archive

Page 63 Gianni Dagli Orti/The Art Archive

Pages 64-65, 65 top Tipical Press Agency/Getty Images

Page 65 bottom Maurice Branger/Roger Viollet/Archivi Alinari, Firenze

Page 66 Hulton-Deutsch Collecion/Corbis

Page 67 Fox Photos/Getty Images

Pages 68-69 Archivi Alinari, Firenze

Page 70 Hulton-Deutsch Collecion/Corbis

Pages 70-71 Imagno/Getty Images

Page 71 Bettmann/Corbis

Page 72 Keystone/Getty Images

Pages 72-73, 74-75 Keystone France/Eyedea/Contrasto

Page 75 top Popperfoto/Getty Images

Page 75 bottom UPPA/Photoshot

Pages 76-77 Time & Life Pictures/Getty Images

Pages 77 top, 77 bottom Mary Evans Picture Library

Page 78 Richard Hewitt Stewart/National Geographic Stock

Pages 78-79 Bettmann/Corbis

Page 80 left Time & Life Pictures/Getty Images

Page 80 right UPPA/Photoshot

Page 81 Volkmar K. Wentzel/National Geographic Stock

Pages 82 top, 82 bottom Keystone/Getty Images

Page 83 James A. Sugar/National Geographic Stock

Page 84 left courtesy of Bertrand Piccard

Page 84 right Herb Swanson

Pages 84-85 courtesy of Bertrand Piccard

Pages 86, 86-87 WpN/UPPA/Photoshot

Page 87 Ho Old/Reuters/Contrasto

Page 88 top Sukree Sukplang/Reuters/Contrasto

Pages 88 bottom, 88-89 Mike Hewitt/Allsport/Getty Images

Pages 90-91 S012/Breitling/Gamma/Eyedea/Contrasto

Page 91 AP/LaPresse

Page 92 Nicolas Le Corre/Gamma/Eyedea/Contrasto

Page 93 top P. Durand/Corbis Sygma/Corbis

Page 93 bottom Nicolas Le Corre/Gamma/Eyedea/Contrasto

Page 94 left Bill Teasdale

Pages 94 center, 94 right, 95 left, 95 right courtesy of the Cameron Balloons

Pages 96-97 courtesy of Tibor Balint, Jet Propulsion Laboratory, NASA

Pages 97 top, 97 bottom courtesy of the NASA

Pages 100-101 Tootie Cadzow

Page 115 left Matthew Wakem/Getty Images

Pages 115 center, 115 right Jean Becker

Page 117 courtesy of Ben Bläss

Pages 126-127 courtesy of Parmigiani Fleurier

Pages 129, 130-131, 133 top, 139, 149, 150-151, 151, 152 top, 152 center, 152 bottom, 152-153, 154, 154-155, 156 top, 156 center, 156 bottom, 156-157, 158 top, 158 bottom, 158-159, 160-161, 161 top, 161 bottom, 162, 163, 164-165, 165 top, 165 bottom Jean Becker

Pages 166-167 Adrian Warren & Dae Sasitorn/www.lastrefuge.co.uk

Pages 170 top, 170-171 Matt Cardy/Getty Images

Pages 172-173, 173 top, 173 bottom Phil Cole/Allsport/Getty Images

Page 176 top Matt Cardy/Getty Images

Page 176 center Graeme Robertson/Getty Images

Page 176 bottom Matt Cardy/Getty Images

Pages 176-177 Adrian Warren & Dae Sasitorn/www.lastrefuge.co.uk

Pages 202-203 courtesy of Ben Bläss

Page 206 Jean Becker

Pages 206-207, 208-209, 209 top, 209 bottom courtesy of Ben Bläss

Page 209 center courtesy of Johan de Jong-www.hotairballoning.nl

Pages 210-211 Jean Becker

Page 211 top courtesy of Johan de Jong-www.hotairballoning.nl

Page 211 bottom courtesy of the Stadsbestuur Sint-Niklaas (Belgium)

Pages 212-213, 214, 215 courtesy of Johan de Jong-www.hotairballoning.nl

Page 216 courtesy of the Stadsbestuur Sint-Niklaas (Belgium)

Pages 216-217 courtesy of Ben Bläss

Page 253 Marcello Libra/Archivio White Star

Page 254 Jean Becker

Page 264 courtesy of Johan de Jong-www.hotairballoning.nl

Pages 268-269 Valentina Giammarinaro

Page 282 top left courtesy of Johan de Jong-www.hotairballoning.nl

ACKNOWLEDGMENTS

The Publisher would like to thank Bertrand Piccard
for his precious help

Jean Becker whishes to thank:
Claude Jelk di Château-d'Oex (Switzerland)
Annette and Didier Sax-Rosseneu from Sint-Niklaas (Belgium)
Muir Moffat and Jane Oakland of Bristol (England)
Philippe Buron Pilâtre and Charlotte Hennequin from Chambley (France)
Don Cameron, hot-air balloons manufacturer Cameron Balloons, Bristol
The pilots, who accompany me: Michel Perrin, Raymond Seigeot, Laurent Boué,
Claude Guittard and Jonathan Becker
My team members: Patrick Dreyer, Romuald Maurice, Jean-Philippe Perraguin, Léo Van Aken,
Guy Mercelat, Philippe Baude, Thierry Cuenat and Marcel Bouwmans,
Josiane Favre and Jean-Marc Jacot from Parmigiani Fleurier (Switzerland)
Yves Ackermann and Serge Tisserand from Conseil Général du Territoire, Belfort (France)
Jeany Lorgeou, mayor of Romorantin (France)
Ulrike Teissier and Frank Farnel from the General Electric of Belfort (France)
Dominique Becker, my wife

304 *An unusually shaped balloon, ready to take off, moves gracefully among the snow-covered pines of the Swiss resort of Château-d'Oex.*

Daniela Comi and Roberto Magni wish to thank:
Paolo and Catherine Barbieri - Comunicazione in Volo
All the pilots who have taken us flying giving us the opportunity to experience new sensations
Kathie Leyendecker and her staff - Albuquerque International Balloon Fiesta, New Mexico (USA)
Charlotte Hennequin and Etienne Tagnon - Lorraine Mondial Air Balloons Chambley (France)
Sophie Guyet - Service press Festival International de Ballons, Château-d'Oex (Switzerland)
Nicky Butcher and his team - Bristol Balloon Fiestas (England)
Achim Schneider - Int. Borkener Ballonfestival/Zippo-Cup (Germany)
Nicole Haggeney - Fire&Snow in Mauterndorf (Austria)
The Organizers of the "Mongolfiere Innamorate" Carpineti (Italy)
The Organizers of the Dolomites Balloon festival (Italy)
The Press Service staff of the Ferrara Balloons Festival (Italy)
Carlo D'Adamo, Luciano Bovina
Canon CPS Italia

WHITE STAR PUBLISHERS

WS White Star Publishers® is a registered trademark
property of Edizioni White Star s.r.l.

© 2009 Edizioni White Star s.r.l.
Via Candido Sassone, 24
13100 Vercelli, Italy - www.whitestar.it

Translation: Gerome Crips - Catherine Howard
Editing: Jane Pamenter - James Morrison

ISBN 978-88-544-0489-2

2 3 4 5 6   15 14 13 12 11

Printed in Indonesia